Drawing Mentor

Volume 11

Still Life Drawing

Volume 12

Landscape Drawing

Volume 13

Portrait Drawing

By Sarah Bowles

ISBN-13: 978-1475035483

ISBN-10: 1475035489

Preface

The *Drawing Mentor* series of books is intended to help beginning to intermediate drawers learn and improve their drawing skills. Each book is written as a stand-alone lesson which can be used on its own, this gives the reader the ability to pick and choose the lessons and skills they would like to learn to the exclusion of all else.

The earlier lessons in the series are very foundational, designed to improve the reader's technical ability and understanding before going on to later lessons which are more project-based and written assuming technical skills have already been developed. If you're an absolute beginner it's recommended that you proceed from Volume 1 as that will ensure your understanding of how to use the techniques employed in later lessons as occasionally these lessons will refer to principles and skills taught in previous volumes.

This book includes Volumes 11, 12 and 13 which are all advanced lessons that use the skills developed in previous volumes to complete finished drawings. Each lesson explains what its specific genre is, some things to take into consideration when drawing in that genre, and then leads you through a step by step example to complete your own drawing. Each step is explained and detailed pictures are provided. Volume 11 focuses on still life drawing, Volume 12 is about landscapes and Volume 13 discusses portraits. (Again, these lessons assume you've already developed fundamental drawing skills. Before attempting it is recommended that you first learn and understand sketching, layout, and how to apply tone, shading and highlights. If you have not developed these skills please refer to previous volumes.)

The intent of the *Drawing Mentor* series is to periodically add new lessons over time to help you continue to improve your skills. If there is a particular skill or lesson you would like covered please feel free to send an email to drawingmentor@gmail.com. Your feedback suggestions and reviews are very much appreciated and will be used to help create lessons that will benefit you the most.

Thanks for choosing *Drawing Mentor*. Here's to your success.

Sincerely,

Sarah Bowles

Help support someone in need.
10% of all profits are donated to organizations
giving humanitarian assistance.

Contents

Portrait Drawing   49

What is a Portrait?   49

Different Styles   50

The Benefits of Portrait Drawing   50

Finding a Model   50

Views   51

Lighting   51

Framing the Portrait   52

A Portrait Tool   52

Results and Comparison   75

Conclusion   76

Still Life

Welcome to Volume 11. The previous ten volumes covered basic drawing and sketching techniques, they are designed to give the reader a solid foundation on which to build as well as the ability to successfully complete the projects presented in any subsequent volume. If you've faithfully read each previous volume and completed all the practice exercises you should've developed a large assortment of drawing skills and the ability to apply them. You should be able to look at an object and make an accurate representation of it on paper using shapes, tone, shading and perspective.

Continuing from this point the majority of volumes will contain project based lessons rather than skill based. They will employ many of the skills you've learned and walk you through projects step by step to completion. Each volume will be different in genre, style or subject. This first project based volume starts with one of the most basic and common art forms, the still life.

Still Life Drawing

Still life drawings and paintings have been done for thousands of years. The ancient Egyptians, Greeks and Romans all had their own style and use for still life images. The techniques have changed over time and have included realistic as well as abstract pieces. A still life drawing is simply a drawing of inanimate objects, or things that no longer move or grow on their own. Common examples of still life subjects are bowls of fruit, cut flowers in a vase, musical instruments, books, rocks and bones. There's no limit to the number of different things you can draw in any particular still life.

Below are some steps/points to keep in mind when setting up a still life. You don't always have to follow them but they'll help you be consistent:

1. Choose an area where you can set up your subject and leave it without it getting disturbed. It may take more than one sitting to finish your drawing. Setting up the subject the exact same way over and over is difficult and tiring. In addition to keeping the subject the same, make sure you can sit in the same spot each time.

2. Choose the items you want to draw. As mentioned before it can be just about anything that won't move while you're drawing it. You can start out with something simple or decide to do something very complex but make sure the subject interests you.

3. Set up the objects so they're stable and won't fall down or shift easily.

4. Make sure you can keep fairly consistent lighting. If the light changes so will the shadows and that can change the whole look of the drawing.

After the setup is complete you must then study it. The chances of successfully creating a finished drawing you're happy with without studying the subject beforehand is very small. For this reason the first step to any still life drawing is to sketch it. The purpose of sketching is to learn how the objects relate to each other in size and position; it's also an opportunity to practice the angles, curves, tone and shading of each object. Sketches don't have to be limited to the subject as a whole. If you're having trouble drawing a particular object correctly, sketch it individually. Studying each particular item as well as the subject as a whole will increase the accuracy of your final piece. In the end, sketching will save a lot of time and frustration and will help you produce a better product.

Once you have your subject set up, have studied and sketched it, you'll be ready to draw a final piece.

The example that follows includes all the required steps for drawing a still life from start to finish. Feel free to follow along by drawing the same still life in this example or, set up your own subject and just follow the steps.

Step by Step Exercise

Setting up the subject is the first thing that needs to be done.

Below is the still life that will be used for this exercise. The objects in the picture were chosen for two reasons. First, their shapes are relatively simple, and second, they have a wide range of characteristics. As you can see, there is a round ball, a shiny black box, a dull white box, a glass vase with plants in it, and a book. The variety of things that can be included is enormous. This example was designed to be fairly simple while still covering many different techniques.

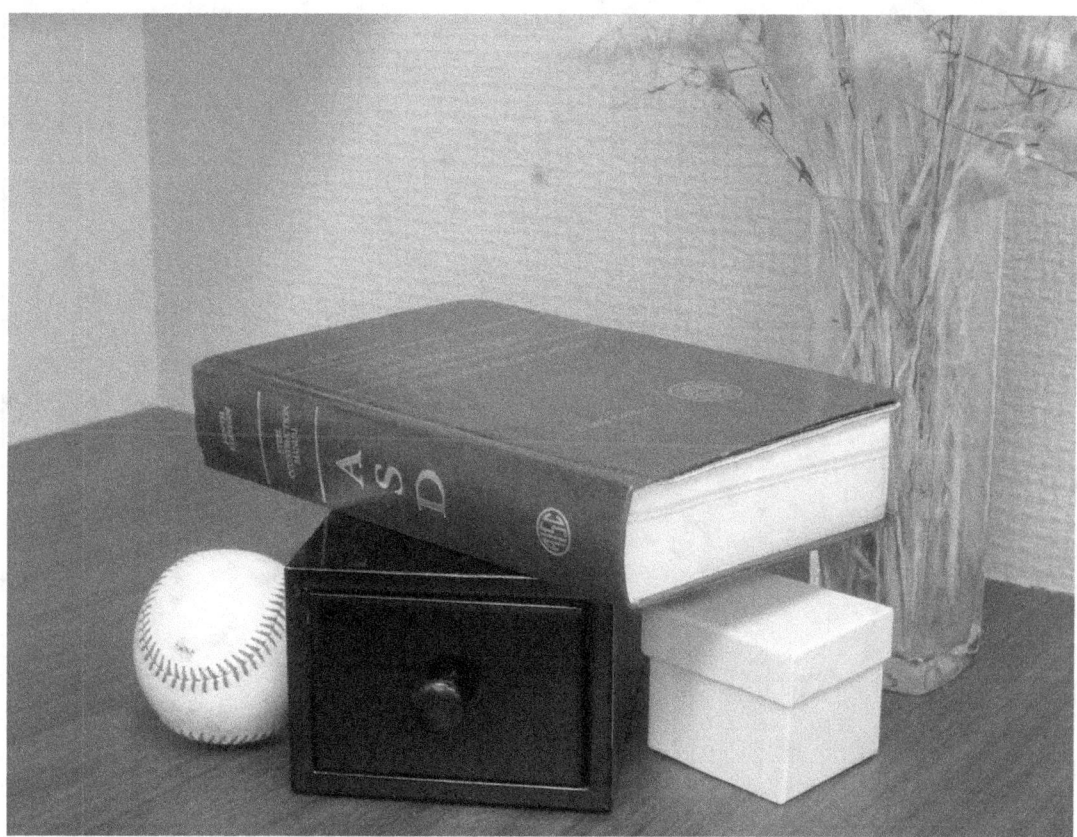

Figure 11-1. Still life setup

Step 2.

Sketch the objects multiple times to become familiar with the layout before starting the final drawing. As you sketch, pay attention to the position and size of each object as it relates to the others, also make sure to observe the tones and shadows. Be aware that each sketch will help you learn. The more you sketch the better you'll know the subject, the more you know about the subject before you begin the easier the final drawing will be.

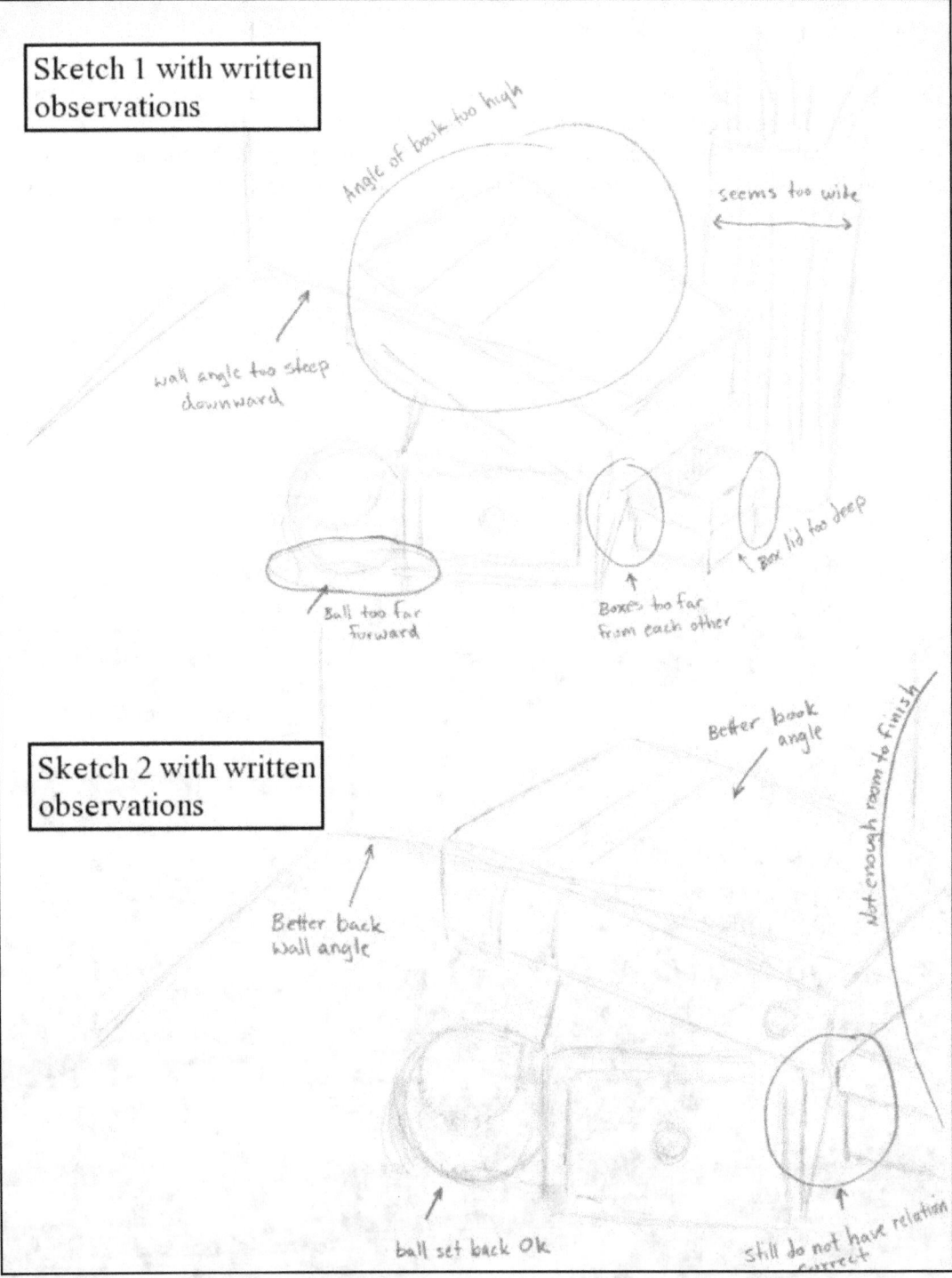

Sketch 1 with written observations

Angle of book too high

seems too wide

wall angle too steep downward

Ball too far forward

Boxes too far from each other

Box lid too deep

Sketch 2 with written observations

Better back wall angle

Better book angle

Not enough room to finish

ball set back ok

still do not have relation correct

Figure 11-2. Initial still life sketches

When you feel you've learned enough through sketching to allow you to accurately lay out the subject, get a piece of paper for the final drawing.

The first thing to do is locate reference points which will help you position all the other objects in their correct place. In this example, the corner created by the wall and desk is a good place to start. Drawing these lines at the correct angle is the key so take the time to get it right. Draw these lines lightly, you may need to adjust them a few times before you get the correct angles and locations, and you may have to erase them later on.

Notice below that the wall does not go straight up and down perfectly vertical; it angles slightly to the left as you draw it up from the corner. Subtle things like this are what you need to be looking for during setup.

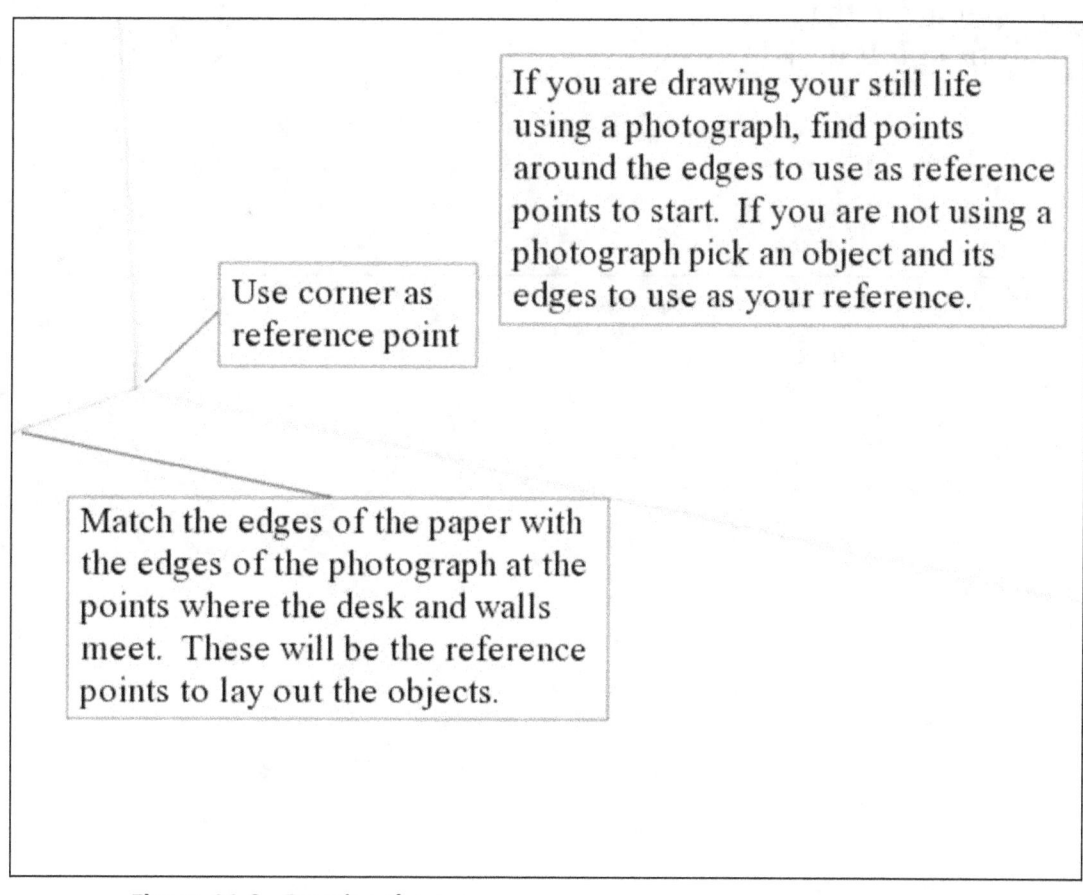

Figure 11-3. Framing the corner

Step 4.

The corner can be used to help locate all the other objects. Start with the objects that cross the line separating the wall and desk. The spine of the book is slightly to the right of the corner and nearly centered along the line that separates the wall and desk. Drawing from left to right the spine of the book slopes down a little steeper than the wall so that the wall line nearly touches the top of the spine on the right side of the book. The top face of the book is not as steep as the left wall line (drawing from left to right).

The vase crosses the desk line on the right side of the picture. The book overlaps a little more than half of the left side of the vase. The rough shapes of the book and the vase should look very similar to the familiar 3-D rectangular shapes discussed in Volume 3.

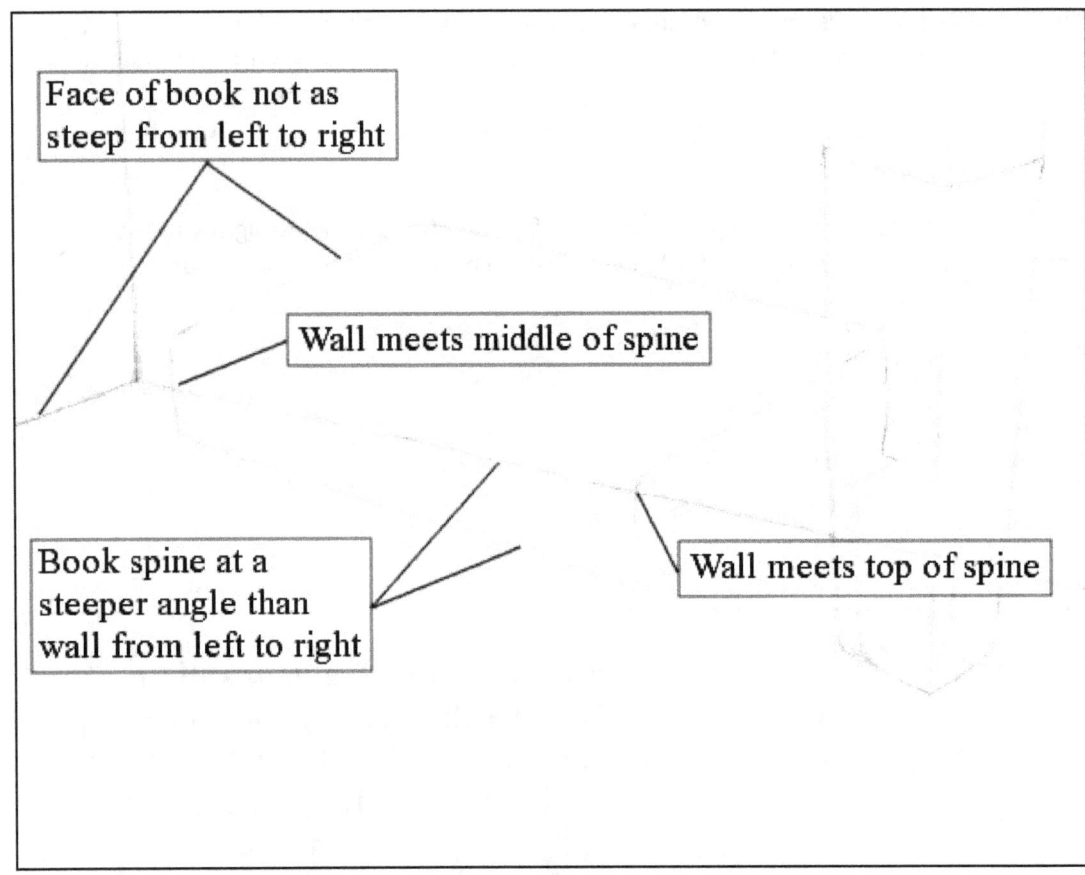

Figure 11-4. Book and vase layout

The black box is the lowest boundary and it's slightly wider than it is tall. There are four things to notice about the black box in the picture. One, you can see three sides of the box. Two, the book is covering part of the upper right corner of the front side. Three, where the book and the box meet in the upper left, the angle they make is acute (less than ninety degrees), and fourth, in the photograph, the bottom of the front of the box slopes down slightly from left to right and the top of the box face should match this slope.

Look at the picture with these four points in mind, then try to match on paper what you see in the picture.

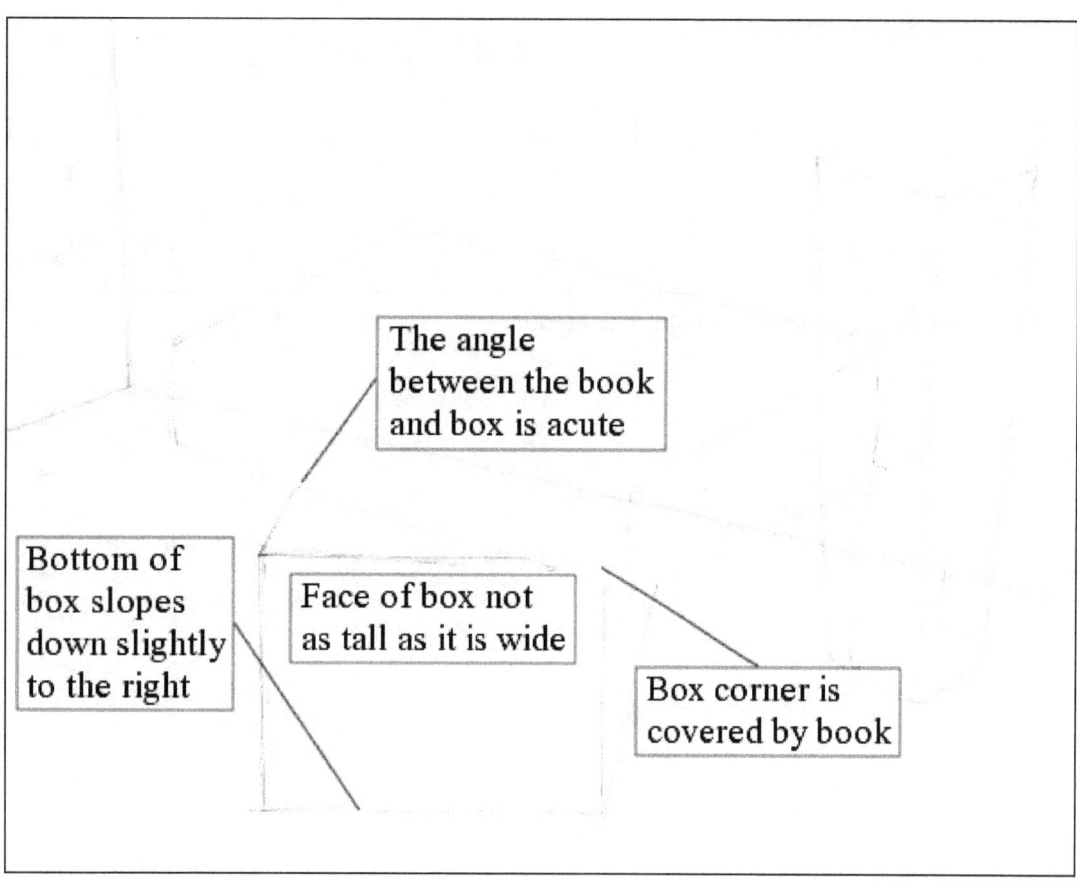

Figure 11-5. Black box layout

Step 6.

The baseball and small box are the last things to lay out. The baseball should start at the upper left corner of the black box and end about one third of the way up from the bottom of the box. For now the baseball is just a circle.

The little white box is made of a few rhombuses. The middle of the right face should cross the bottom of the vase. The angle of the right face nearly matches the angle of the right face of the vase. The bottom corner of the box should be nearly in line with the lower left corner of the black box. Notice the white box does not touch the black one and that the white box is just tall enough that the book covers the top left side.

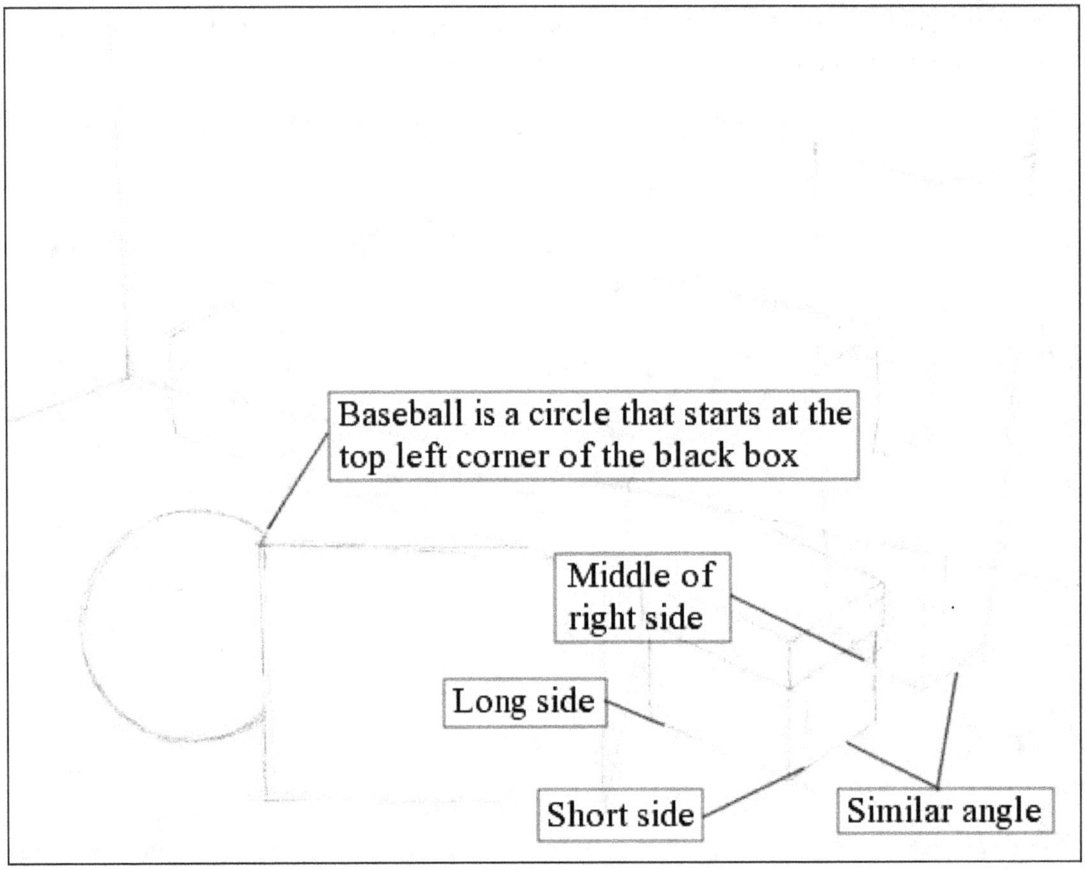

Baseball is a circle that starts at the top left corner of the black box

Middle of right side

Long side

Short side

Similar angle

Figure 11-6. Ball and white box layout

Add guidelines for the interior details like the stitching on the baseball, the thickness of the book cover and the rim and handle of the black box.

Erase the lines you don't need and make the final adjustments to the shapes of each object.

This is the final step before applying tone; it's also the time to double check the layout you've drawn against the subject. Make sure they match because from this point on, the rest of the drawing process consists of adding tone; it's a lot harder to erase tone than layout lines. Take the time to make sure you have everything in its proper place and at the proper angle.

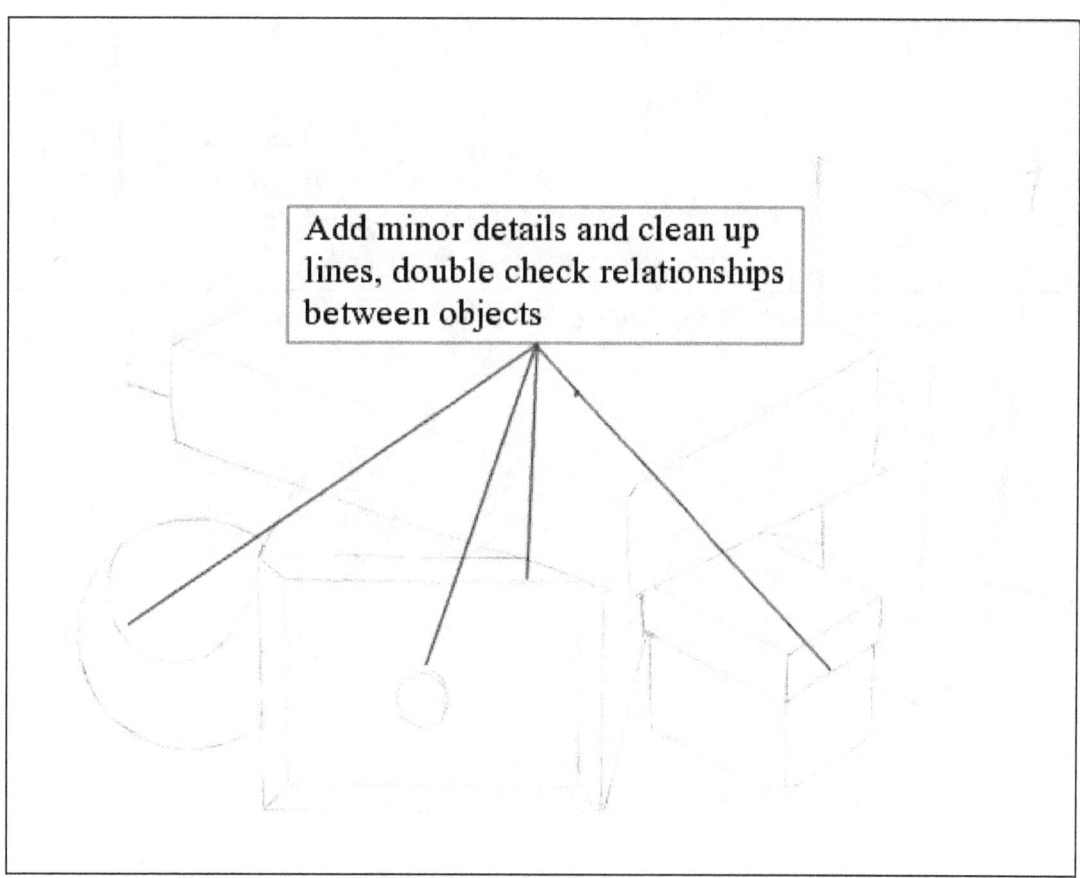

Add minor details and clean up lines, double check relationships between objects

Figure 11-7. Final layout of objects, minor detail lines added

Step 8.

Now that the layout is complete, tone and shading can be added.

The first layer of tone you add can be very rough, it mainly gives you something to work on; still, this is a good time to begin developing relative depths of tone between the objects.

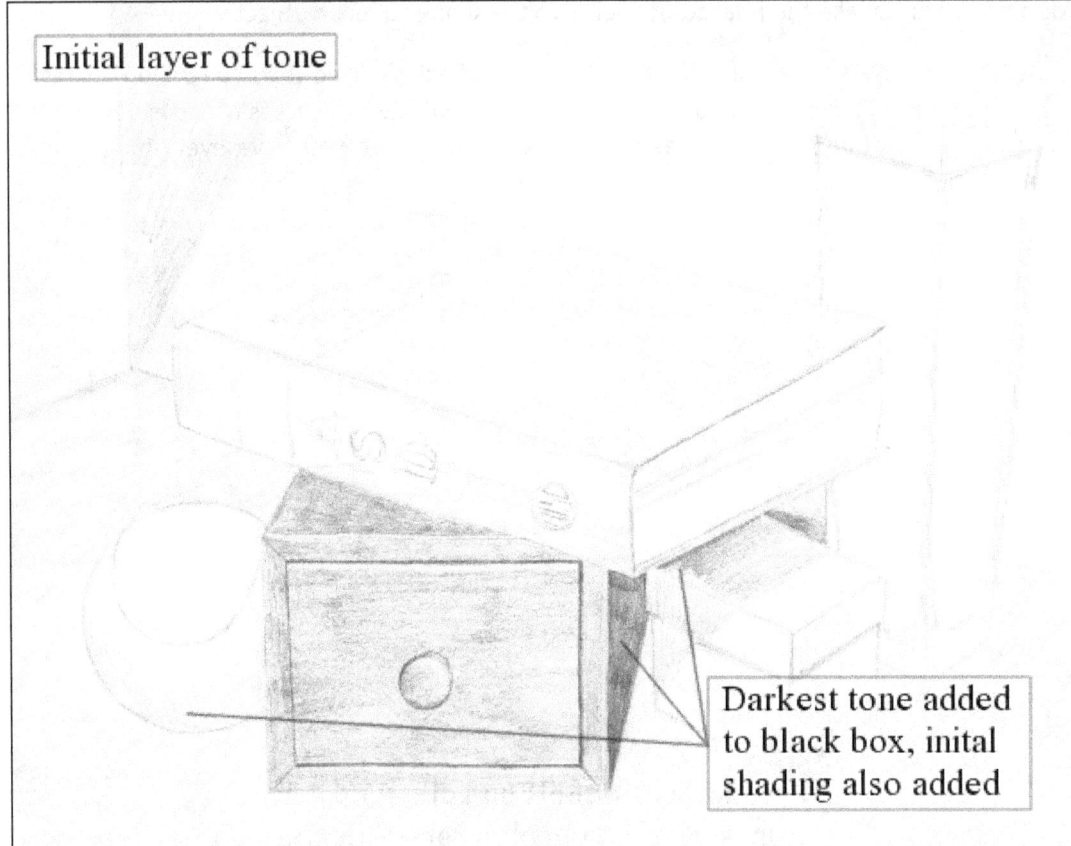

Initial layer of tone

Darkest tone added to black box, inital shading also added

Figure 11-8. Initial tone, shading and details

Place the darkest tone on the black box. Add the major shadows to the white box and some shading to the underside of the baseball. The desk and walls should also be given an initial layer of tone. The writing on the cover and spine of the book is added at this point however some of it is eliminated later on. It's okay to omit or eliminate details, especially if they aren't important and you feel it will improve the quality of the final drawing.

Using a folded piece of paper, a tissue or a tortillon, blend the initial layer of tone. After the tone has been blended, build upon it by adding more layers of tone. Continue the process of adding and blending tone until the tone of each object is fully developed.

The black box of course is very dark but don't just go crazy filling it all in as black as you can because even something completely black will have light and dark areas. Looking around the seams of the drawer and some of the edges you'll see highlights and dark shadows. It'll be easier to finish the highlights if you leave these areas white.

Add ambient shadows around the baseball, to the right of the black box, and along the back wall.

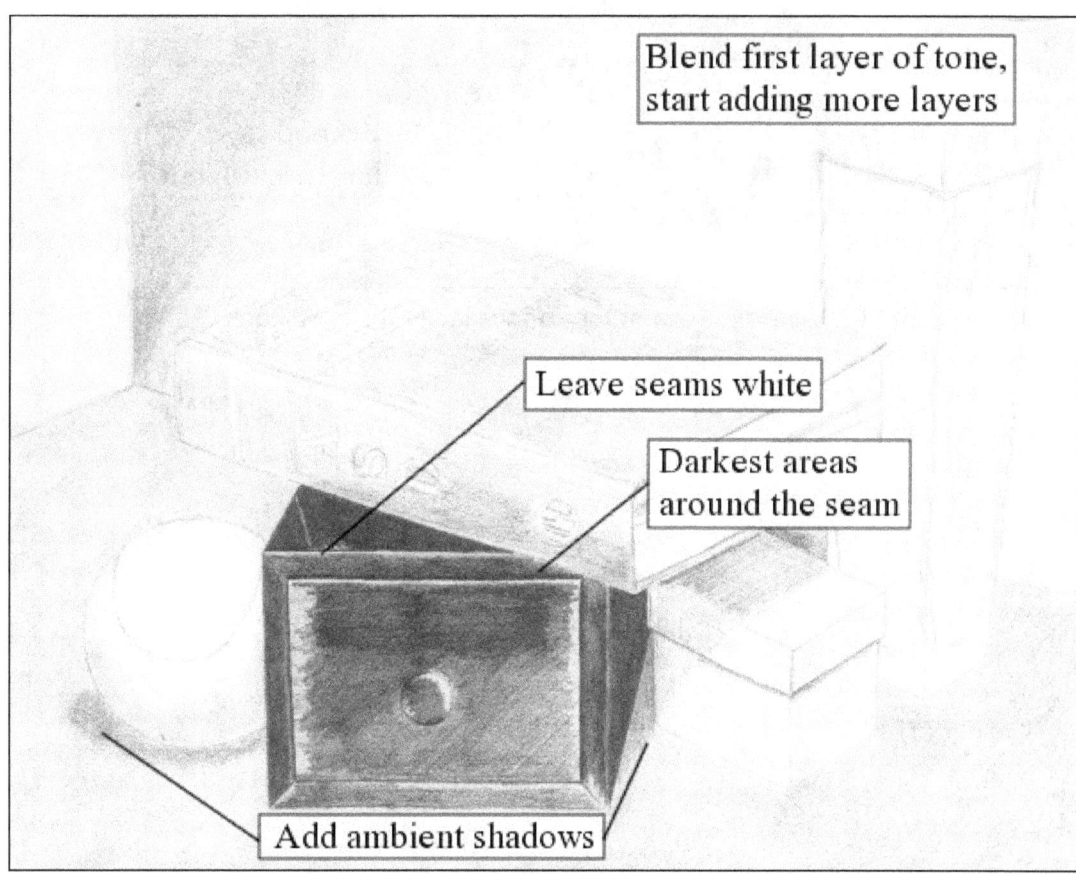

Figure 11-9. Initial layer of tone blended, second layer started

Step 10.

Continue deepening and blending the tone on the black and white boxes and the book. Add stitching to the ball and another layer of tone on the back wall.

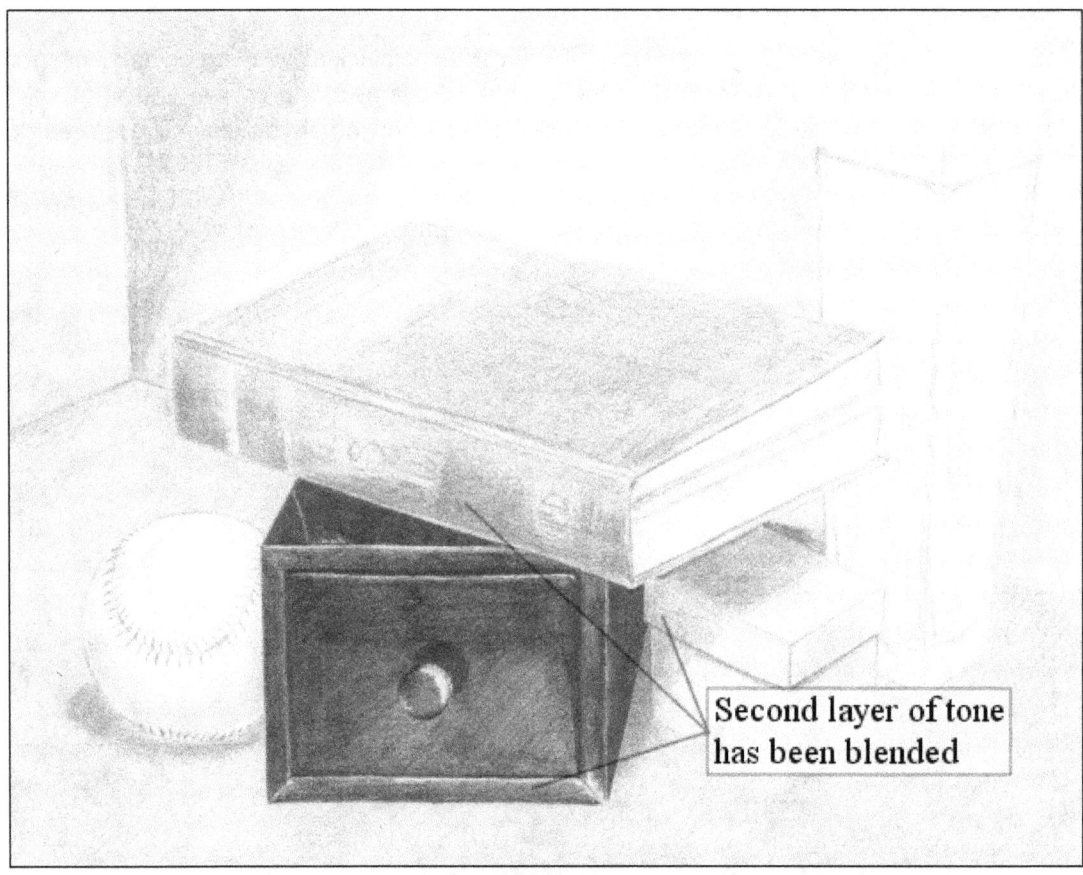

Second layer of tone has been blended

Figure 11-10. Second layer of tone on the boxes, ball and book

Take a moment to stop and compare your drawing to the subject; by now you may start seeing differences between the two. Make corrections to the tone of the objects as needed and blend the tone to get good uniform coverage over each surface.

Take time with this step, think of it as a checkpoint. If you don't like how things are turning out, you're still at a point where you haven't invested a lot of time; it's not too late to start over. From this point on the rest of the process consists of perfecting tones, shadows and details, so if you don't like your start you probably won't like the finish no matter what you do. Starting over isn't the worst thing in the world. Since you've already attempted the drawing once, a second setup will be much faster and more accurate. Use what you've learned from the first setup to make the second one better.

Notice below that the writing on the front cover of the book is now gone and the overall tone of the book is darker and more uniform. Also, look at the relationship that's starting to develop between the book and the black box. A book is not something typically thought of as being reflective but the darker area on the spine of the book is actually a reflection of the black box, the lighter area under the letter "A" is the reflection of the baseball.

The shadows on the white box have also been softened and blended.

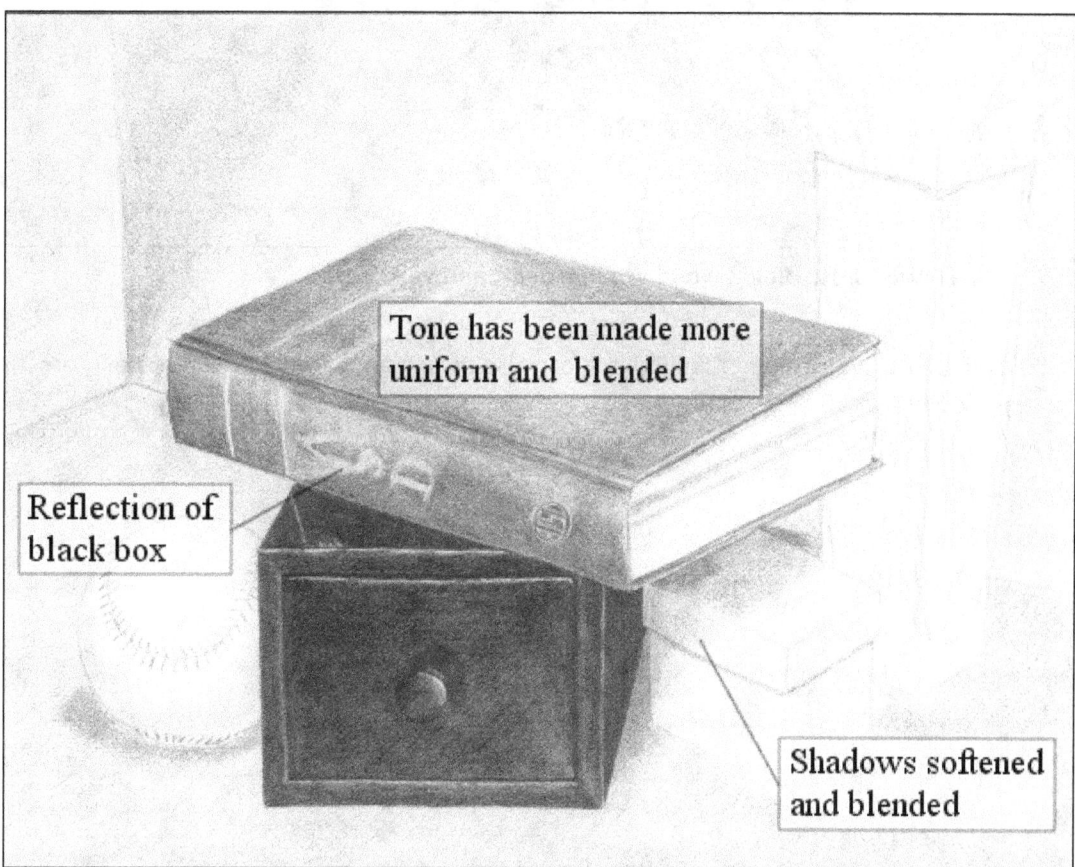

Figure 11-11. Second layer of tone complete

Step 12.

Begin adding the minor details starting with the wood grain in the desk. Wood grain can be added a couple ways. You can either draw a continuous line for each division, or use many small lines following the contours of the grain, similar to hatching.

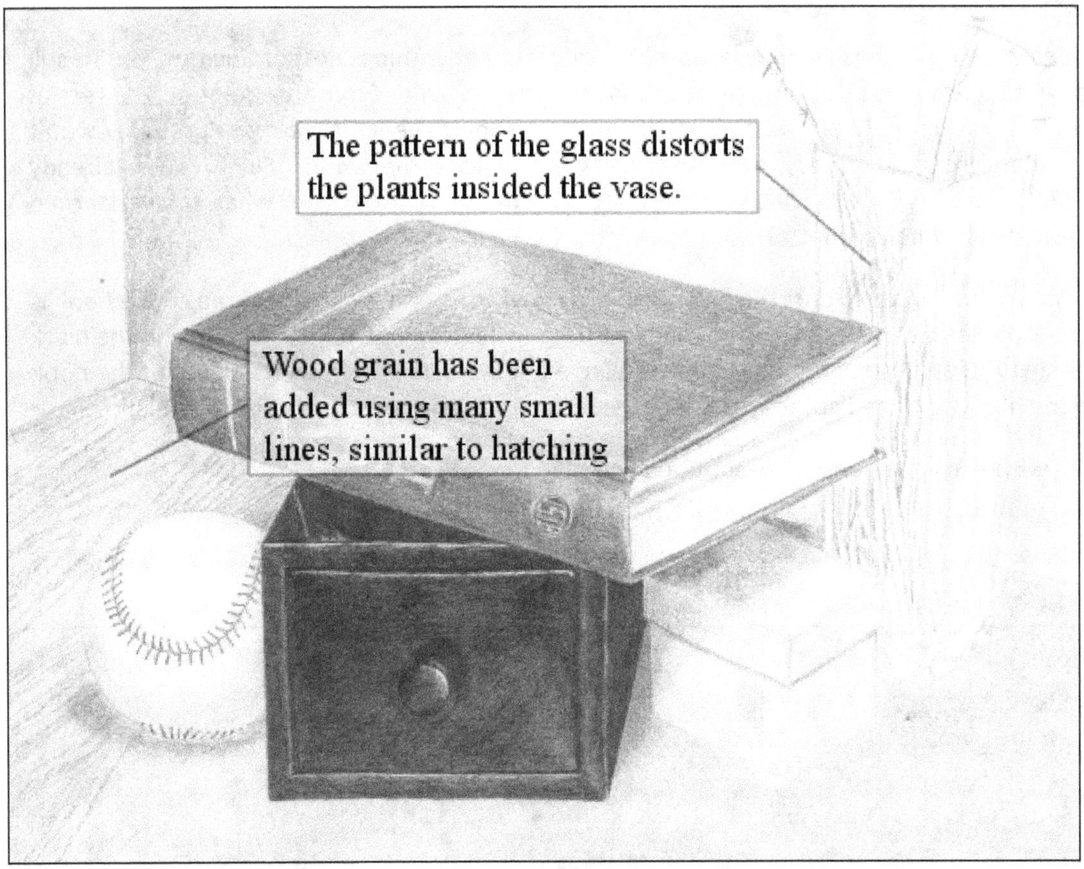

The wood grain in the photo is not very distinct but the pattern is made from many small line segments. The grains of wood in the drawing have been drawn similarly (using hatching), however they were spaced a little farther apart for clarity and speed.

In addition to the desk, begin detailing the vase. The glass of the vase is wavy. Because of the wavy pattern the plants inside appear wavy and distorted as well. Glass is an interesting material because it can mimic the colors of what's inside or behind it, it can also distort appearances and create interesting highlights.

The pattern of the glass distorts the plants insided the vase.

Wood grain has been added using many small lines, similar to hatching

Figure 11-12. Begin wood grain in desk, and vase detail

Step 13.

Continue adding the wood grain pattern until you've covered the whole desk. Some of the wood grains should go all the way across the desk, some of them should turn back on themselves and reverse direction (this indicates that the wood wasn't cut parallel to the wood grain).

Lightly blend the initial tones in the vase. Try to match the tones of whatever is in and behind it. In this case most of the vase will match the tone of the wall and plants. The bottom, corners, and rim at the top tend to remain highlighted, keep those areas lighter for now.

Blend the shadows of the objects into the tone of the desk.

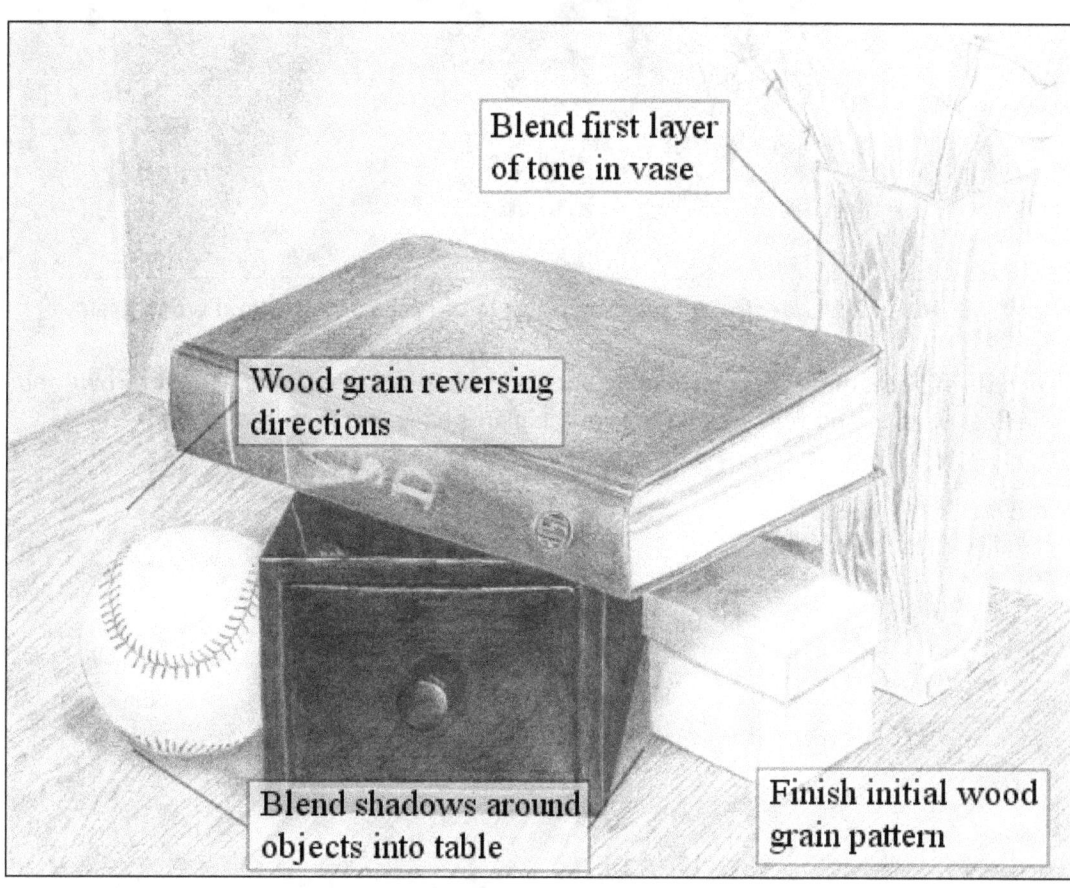

Figure 11-13. Finish initial wood grain and vase details

Step 14.

The next step takes some extra time and consideration. The back wall has a complex woven pattern in it. Before adding it, take time to study it. Determine which areas are highlighted, which are shaded, and how the pattern repeats itself. You'll see that the wall has a base tone and small variations in shading can be used to describe the pattern. Sketch the pattern a few times on a scratch piece of paper to determine if you want to add it and how you're going to do it. You can omit the pattern if you want, but it is a good challenge.

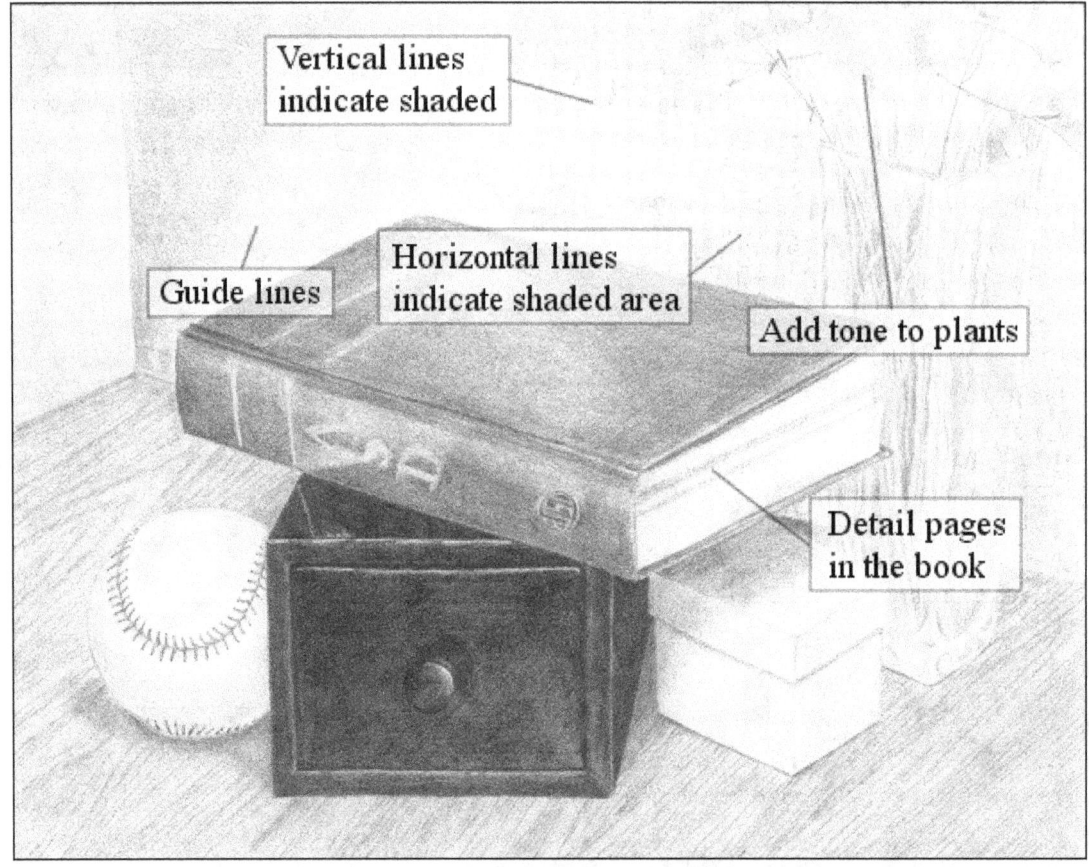

Figure 11-14. Begin wall pattern, finish initial vase detail, blend wood grain

This is one part of the drawing where a ruler would be handy. Using a ruler you can add guidelines to help keep the rows and columns of the weave straight. The pattern really only consists of slight differences in shading but they're laid out in definite, straight, rows and columns. In addition to the back wall, the book pages and tops of the plants have also received more detailing.

Finish laying out the weave pattern on the wall.

When you've finished the weave it'll be easier to add more detail to the plants above the vase. Look at the plants in the picture and notice the different sizes, thicknesses and tones of the stems.

Plants can usually be drawn a little more freely than other objects because they're organic and not as rigid as most man-made things. You can be a little more relaxed here but still try to maintain some accuracy. The fuzzy balls can be drawn with a base tone layer followed by some thin dark lines and thin highlights radiating from the center.

Another layer of tone was also added to the black box.

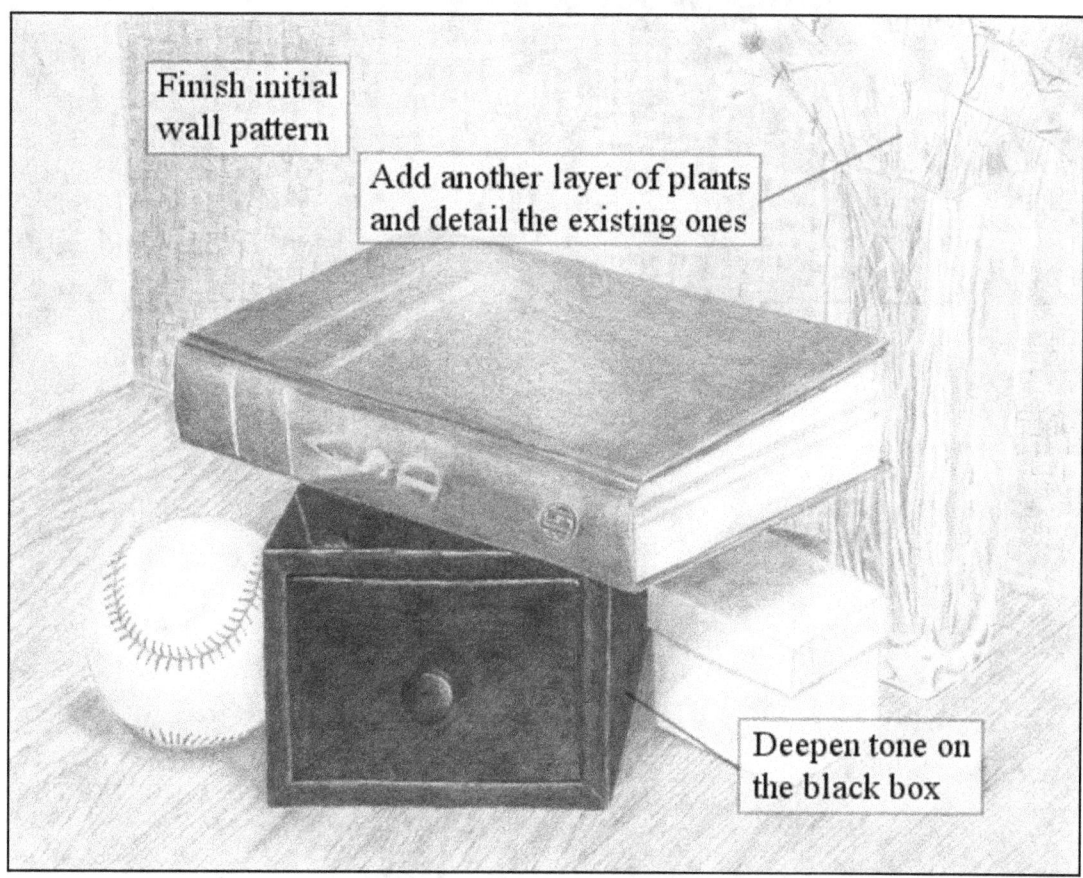

Figure 11-15. Finish wall pattern layout, deepen tone on black box and vase

Step 16.

Everything is now basically laid out and ready for final detailing.

This is another good point to take a long look at the subject. Really focus on the depth of tone and make

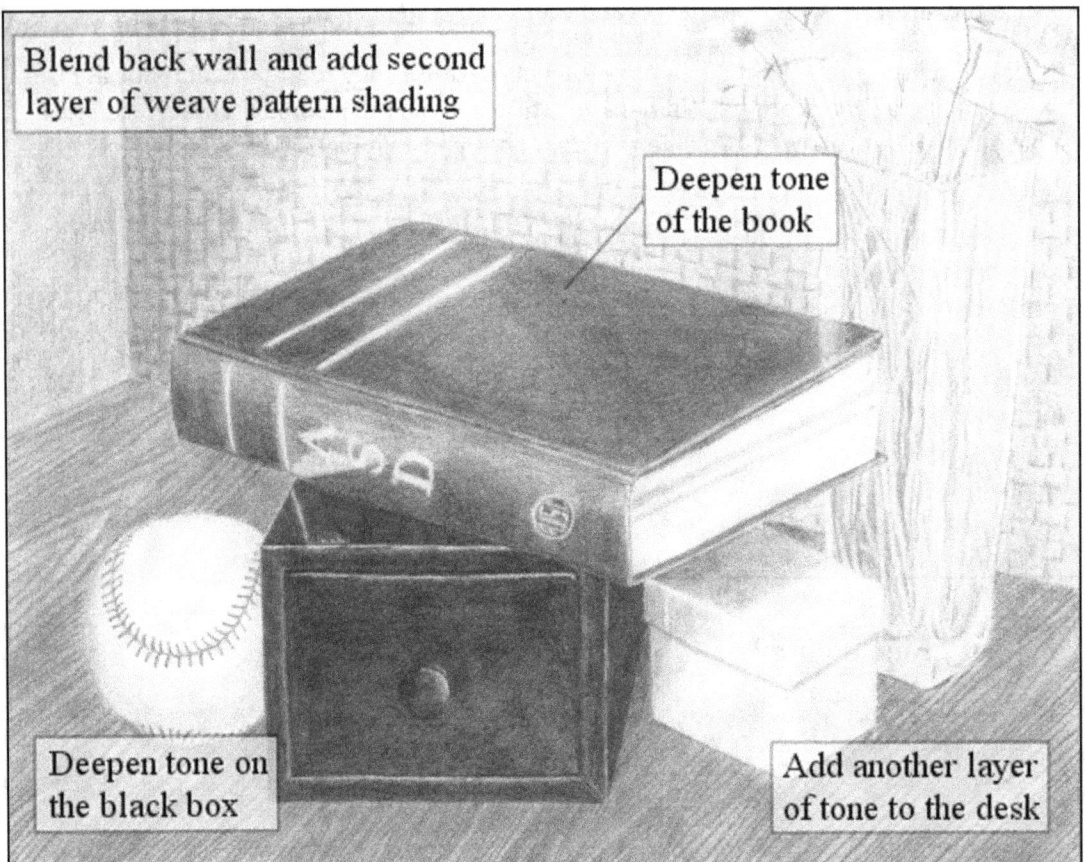

Blend back wall and add second
layer of weave pattern shading

Deepen tone
of the book

Deepen tone on
the black box

Add another layer
of tone to the desk

Figure 11-16. Deepen all tones as needed

sure the tones of your drawing are correct. It's obvious from Step 15 that the desk and the book needed another layer of tone. To deepen the tone of the desk, draw another set of wood grain lines over the first and smudge them into the surface. Add more tone to the book and blend it as well.

Blend the initial layer of tone on the walls and begin to refine the pattern of the back wall. Add another layer of tone to the black box.

At this point most of the tone is good but still rather rough. Blend the tone well so it's consistent and the shadows very smooth. Use an eraser to clean up the edges and add highlights to the objects.

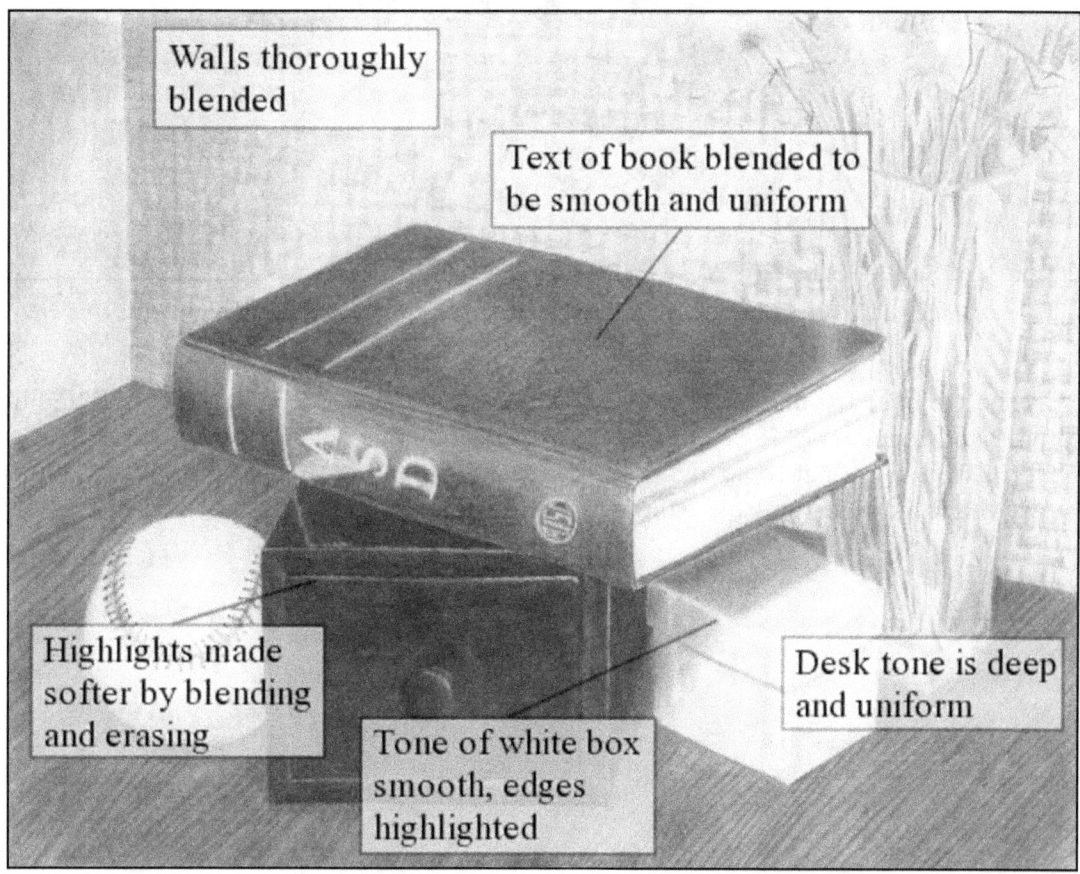

Figure 11-17. Blend all tone thoroughly to create smooth uniform surfaces, begin to add highlights

Step 18.

The last step is strictly finishing touches which can actually take a very long time. The level of detail achieved depends on the person drawing.

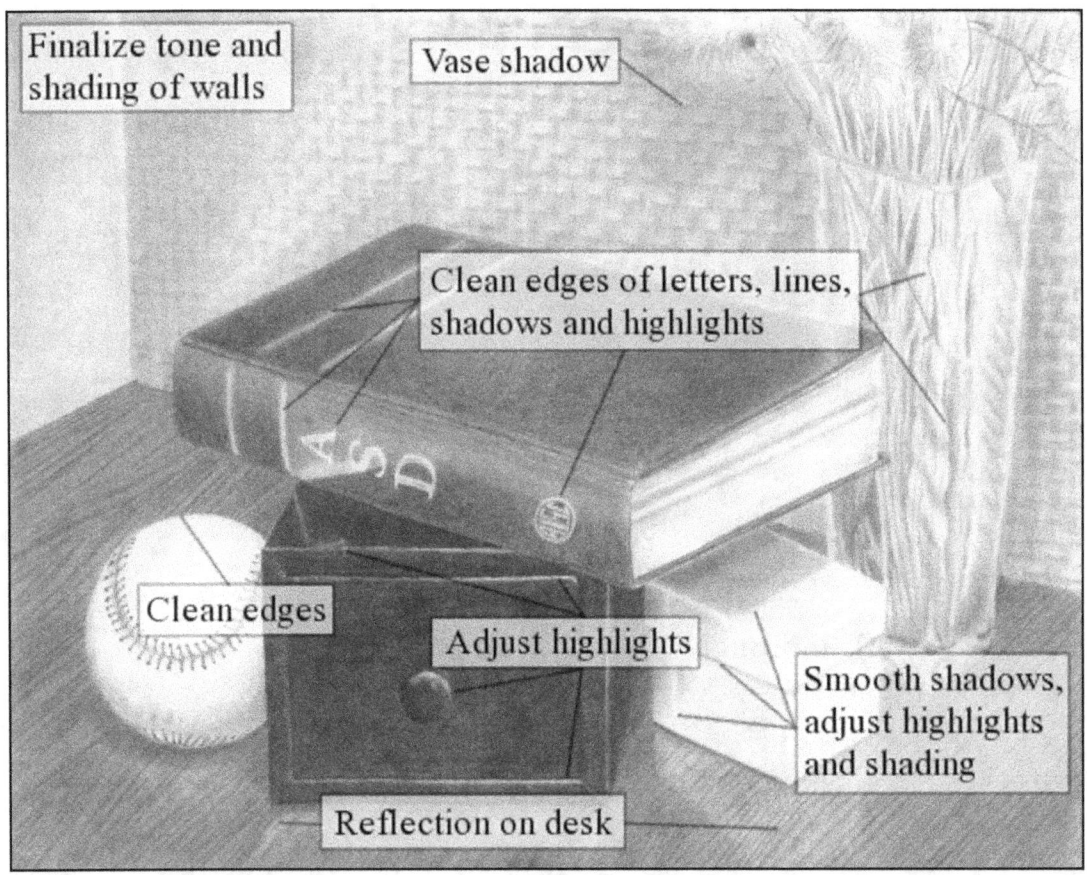

In this example the back wall was finished by deepening and blending the tone of the shaded areas in the weave pattern, and by adding a shadow behind the vase. The overall tone of the vase was darkened to match the tone of the wall better, and more shadows in and around the plants were added. Highlights were then cleaned up with an eraser.

Figure 11-18. Completed drawing after final adjustments and highlights

An eraser was also used to show the reflections of the boxes and ball by removing tone from the desk. Take a second to notice the difference in the appearance from Step 17 to Step 18 with all the highlights completed and the edges cleaned up. The highlights seem to bring out a whole new dimension to the drawing. The drawing in Step 17 looks very flat compared to the drawing in Step 18 with highlights added. You can see that highlighting really helps a drawing look more three dimensional.

Results

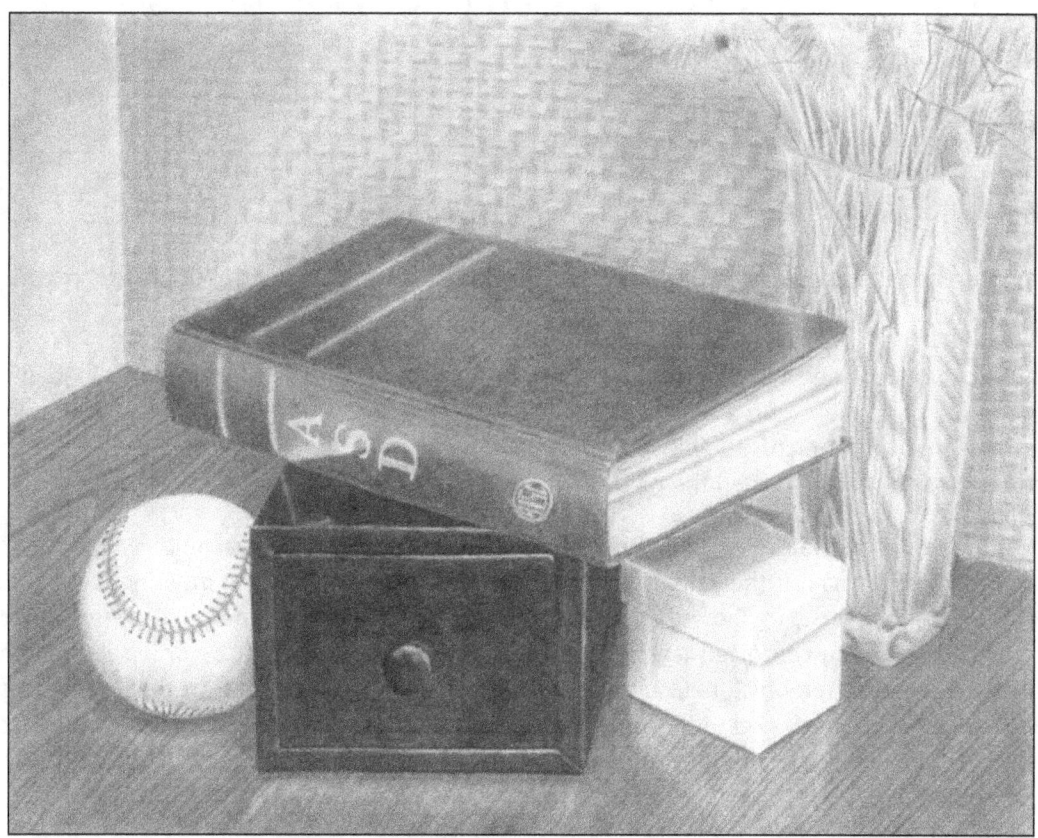

Figure 11-19. Final still life drawing

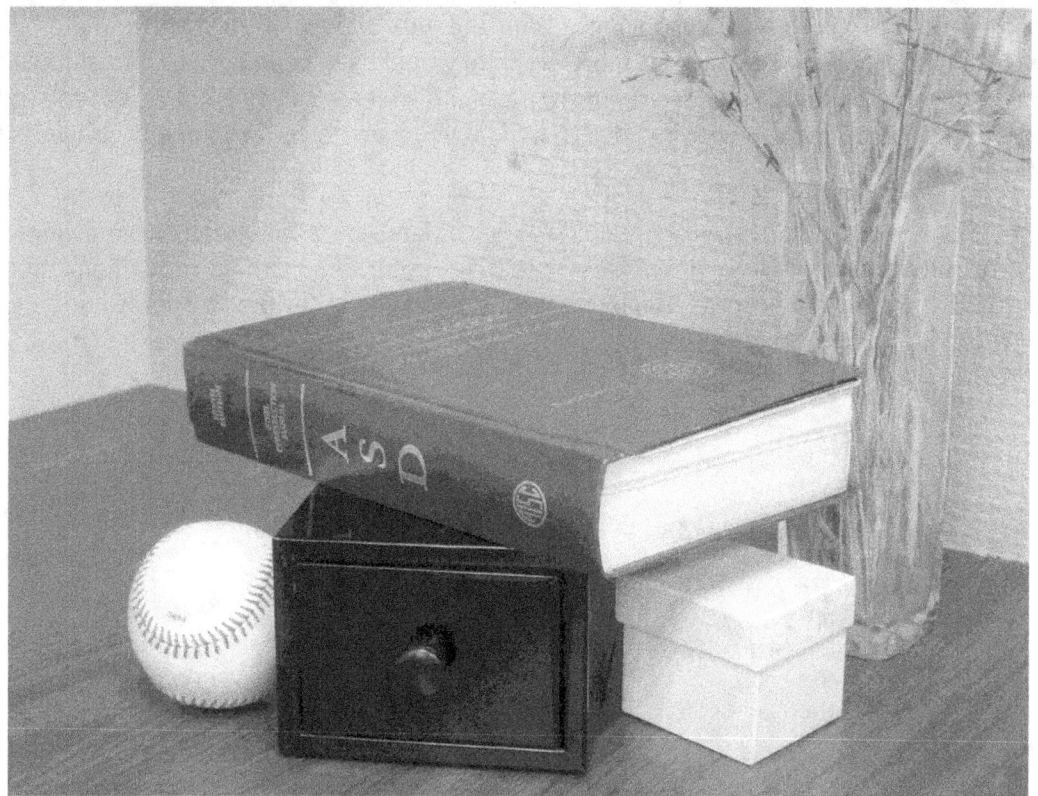

Figure 11-20. Still life photograph

Conclusion

Congratulations you have now finished Volume 11 and the first of the project lessons.

The previous page is a comparison of this lesson's still life drawing versus the original photograph. It's easy to see there are differences between the two. Let's discuss three of the most obvious.

First and most noticeable, the view angle of the two pictures is different. Look at the shape of the book cover and the top of the white box. It's easy to see that the rhombuses that make up these objects in the drawing are taller than the ones in the picture. This indicates that the artist's eyes when the drawing was laid out were higher than the lens of the camera when the picture was taken.

Second, the pattern on the back wall is different. When the wall pattern was initially laid out (see Step 14), it became apparent that it was not the same as the pattern in the picture but the drawing was finished with this error for a couple reasons. First, to show that when viewed by itself without the picture next to it, it looks just fine, and second, because you can often learn more by making a mistake than by doing it right the first time. You'll remember mistakes better which helps you to not repeat them in the future. If that wall were to be drawn again it would be done with much greater accuracy and speed because lessons have been learned from making a mistake. In order to fully avoid these types of errors, sketches should be done of each component of a scene as was mentioned in Step 2.

Third, the tone of the drawing is not as dark as the picture. There are a few things that influenced the depth of the tone. If a different pencil had been used, say a 6B, a deeper tone would have been achieved. A different type of paper may also have been able to hold more tone and look darker. Using a softer material to blend the tone may have also achieved a darker result as more graphite would have been pushed into all the little cracks of the paper. Lastly, the method used to convert a drawing to a digital format may not be able to pick up the full depth of tone. This is something you need to keep in mind if you plan on converting your drawings into a digital format for online viewing.

Even though there are differences between the drawing and the photograph the drawing is still a good representation of the still life and the differences have been used as a learning tool. Remember, a drawing doesn't have to match the picture or scene exactly for it to be good and for others to appreciate it.

Hopefully you had fun with this project. The next volume will cover the topic of landscapes.

Landscapes

Welcome to Volume 12 where we will discuss the topic of landscapes. When you've completed this volume you should know what a landscape is, where you can find them, and some principles to keep in mind as you draw them. You will also have an opportunity to draw a landscape yourself as you go through the step by step example.

So what is a landscape? Usually when one hears the word landscape they tend to think of scenes of wide valleys with mountains in the background or fields of grass and flowers, perhaps trees along a river or lake and maybe even animals; if that's what comes to your mind then you're on the right track.

The simplest explanation of a landscape is that it depicts the land on which we live whether it's several thousand acres or just a few. Mountains, valleys, fields, water, vegetation, the sky and clouds are all important elements of landscapes. The balance of these features is what gives the landscape its mood.

Landscape art has been practiced by many cultures throughout history. The Chinese tradition of landscape art is very ancient. The Romans painted landscapes on the walls of their homes as decoration. In Europe, landscape art didn't start to develop until the 15th century, but at the time it was mainly used just for background purposes.

The Dutch made landscape art a category of its own between the 16th and 17th centuries.

In the United States the frontier became a popular subject starting in the mid 1800's with the organization of the Hudson River School.

Some artists consider man-made structures like roads and buildings acceptable components of a landscape, believing that adding those elements helps to better portray the world we live in. Others argue that a true landscape should only depict nature in its original condition without the influence of people. You're free to decide what you think should be included.

Many animals do what they can to create comfortable living conditions and people are no different. Roads, buildings and people can add variety and interest but as the focus of a drawing switches from the land and nature more towards buildings and roads it gets classified into a subcategory of landscapes, the cityscape. A cityscape shares many characteristics of a landscape but there will usually be a greater dependence on using perspective (see Volume 3).

Drawing a Landscape

Once you've decided to draw a landscape there are three ways to acquire a subject.

The first is to go outside and just draw what you see wherever you are. You can sit outside your house, go to a park, or travel out into the country or wilderness.

When drawing a landscape from real life observation it may help to use a viewfinder to frame your picture. A viewfinder is basically a piece of tag-board with a rectangle cut out of the center; the rectangle represents the surface of your paper. You use it by holding it up in front of you and drawing what you see through it.

If you're outside be prepared for the weather. Rain can be a problem so you may need some kind of cover. Drawing on loose paper on a windy day is also challenging. Sketchbooks work well outside, the paper is usually thicker and more rigid and you won't have to carry a hard surface with you.

Keep in mind that as the sun moves across the sky, shadows change. This can make it difficult to draw outside unless you do it quickly. Sometimes it's better to sketch the scene and possibly take a few photos (maybe even from different locations), then take it all home to use to make your final drawing.

The Second way to acquire a subject is to use pictures and photographs. They can be pictures you take or pictures found in books, magazines and online. There are advantages and disadvantages to this method. One advantage is that weather isn't a factor; another is that it eliminates the need for a viewfinder because the picture and perspective are already set. This is also one of the disadvantages, it's good to frame your own pictures and determine perspective from time to time; relying solely on pictures won't allow you to develop that skill.

If you use a picture that includes a building, find the vanishing points by extending lines from the walls and roof (see Volume 10). This is good practice in general but will also help you understand the perspective of the landscape.

The last way to draw a landscape is from your mind. Before you do this, it's helpful to do many drawings from real life and pictures to develop a solid understanding of perspective and how tone and details change depending on location. Drawing from real life first will also help you develop your own techniques for drawing all sorts of outdoor elements like trees, bushes, grass, rocks, people, animals and buildings.

After drawing enough landscapes from observation, drawing a landscape from your head will be simple and fun.

Layout Tips

Before beginning the step by step exercise, here are a few tips to keep in mind when doing your own drawing. It's important to understand these rules; they'll help you create a more balanced drawing (for examples of many of these tips see Volume 6).

Don't draw the horizon line in the middle of the paper so the drawing is half ground and/or water, and half sky. It may sound strange but dividing the paper in half like this will make the drawing look unbalanced. Your paper shouldn't have two equal areas of tone. One major area of tone should be larger than the other.

Avoid symmetry. This rule goes right along with the one above it. Equal areas of tone, top to bottom, left to right, or diagonal will not be appealing to look at and won't feel balanced. Make sure there is at least one area that gives more tonal weight to either the light or dark tones. It's also recommended to avoid symmetry when placing objects like trees, rocks, and mountains.

Avoid placing the focus of the drawing in the exact center. The main focus might be a tree, a house, an animal or anything else but don't draw it in the center of the paper; locate it slightly to the left or right and possibly slightly up or down too.

Similar to the last rule, avoid creating lines that converge in the center. A road or building should not have lines that end in the center of the picture, they need to be offset similar to how the main subject is offset.

Draw lines that lead the viewer's eyes toward the center. This rule may seem to contradict the previous two but there's good reason for it. You want the viewer's eyes to stay on the picture and not be led off the page. Remember that eyes follow lines. Lines that come close or point to the center without touching it keep the viewer's eyes on the picture. For example, a road could be drawn such that it angles towards the center and goes over a hill and out of sight near the center. A mountain side can be drawn so that if the line continued it would come close to passing through the center. A building could be situated close to the center, or a group of trees could taper towards the center of the drawing. There are many ways to point to the center without actually drawing lines to it or objects on it.

Remember to leave extra space around the focus of the drawing. Don't make the subject so big that it crowds the edges of the paper.

Last of all, don't make a drawing using only horizontal lines. Horizontal lines make a drawing feel calm, almost boring, if your drawing has a lot of horizontal lines and surfaces it will seem boring too. Remember this about lines, horizontal lines create a peaceful, resting, calm feeling, vertical lines create a feeling of stability, and diagonal lines create a feeling of movement. It's important to understand this principle so that you can add lines in a way that will create interest and balance.

Step by Step Exercise

The exercise that follows is a step by step example of the process of drawing a landscape. To break it down into three simple steps it goes as follows:

First, draw a number of practice sketches to gain a general understanding of the landscape features and to determine a balanced layout.

Next draw a simple line layout of the major landscape features.

Finally, build up layers of tone and finish by adding the minor details, shading and highlights.

Feel free to follow along using the same picture as the example, one of the other pictures provided or a picture you find on your own.

Choose a landscape.

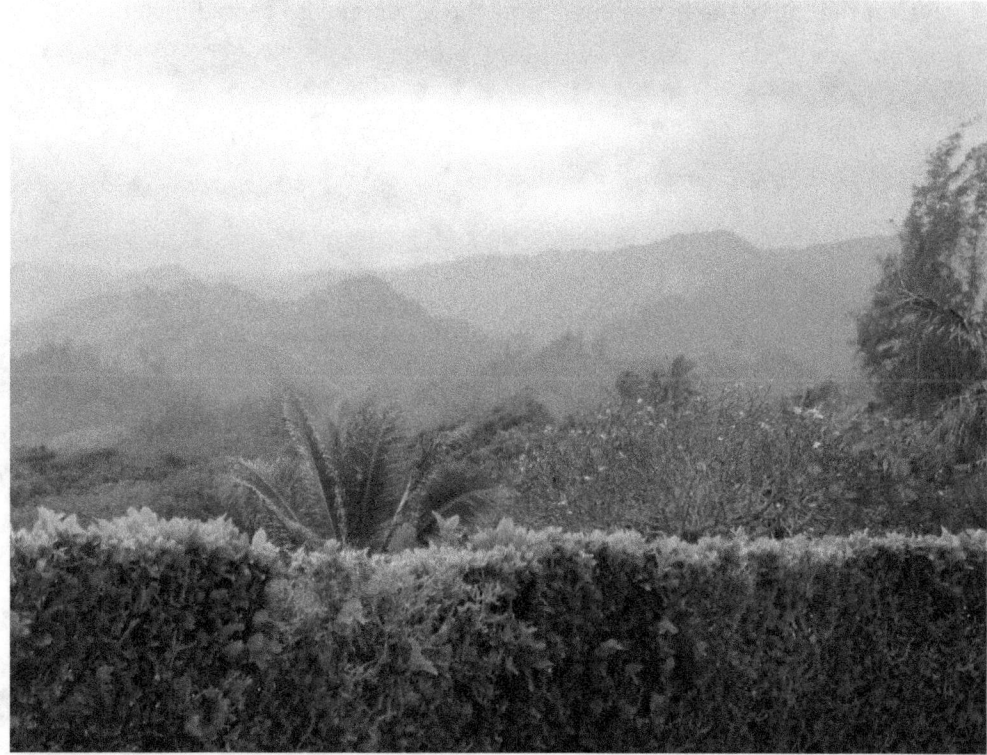

Figure 12-1. Tropical landscape

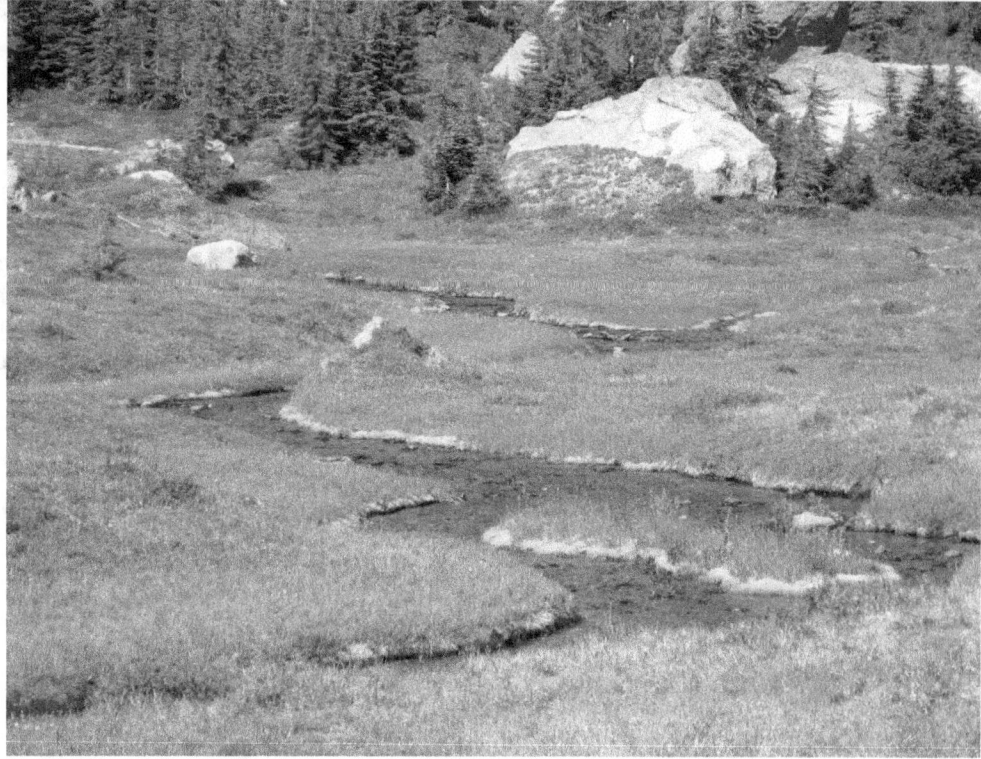

Figure 12-2. Mountain stream

Figure 12-1 is a relatively simple landscape. The large majority of the work consists in the mountains and clouds which are various shades of gray with very little detail. The clouds are interesting because even though they're gray, it's also the location of the brightest highlights. There are some minor details in the fern and the leaves at the top of the hedge but overall this landscape isn't too difficult.

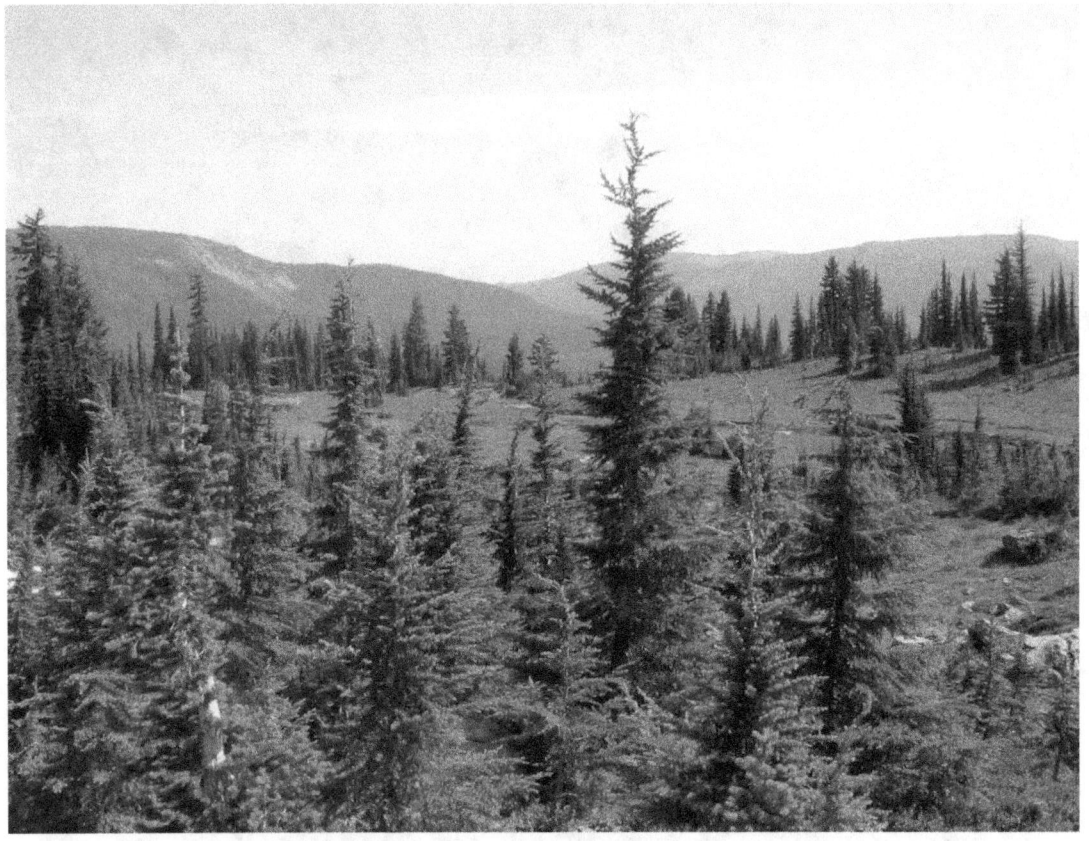

The landscape in Figure 12-2 is more complex than the tropical landscape of Figure 12-1. There's no sky but there are a few trees with large contrasts in tone. The rocks will be the brightest areas as parts of them are almost white. The water is dark blue and should be one of the darkest areas in the drawing aside from the shadows in the trees. Except for a few areas around the edges, the water doesn't reflect much of what's around it because the surface is broken by ripples. The moss along the stream's edge is much lighter than the grass behind it and will almost act like a highlight. The grass in the field has a fairly consistent tone and texture with various patches either darker or lighter. Overall this scene isn't too complicated however there's enough small detail that it could take a considerable amount of time to include it all.

Figure 12-3. Mountain forest landscape

The mountain forest landscape in Figure 12-3 above was chosen for the example in this exercise. This scene can be rather challenging because of the amount of detail in the trees. It's not necessary or even feasible in most cases to include every detail of every tree and techniques can be used to simplify the drawing (see Volume 8), even so this scene may require a significant amount of time to complete. Feel free to use one of the other two examples or one of your own choosing, and just follow the steps. If you choose to follow the example but don't want to spend time adding minute details to so many trees you can draw just a portion of the scene rather than the whole thing.

Study the landscape by sketching the overall layout as well as specific characteristics. Below are some sketches and studies done for the chosen landscape; they explore the overall layout of the picture as well as some of the details. Details included in the sketches below include the relationship of tone between the mountains and sky, a few of the main trees and background trees, and some of the larger rocks.

Sketching the landscape characteristics helps you get a feel for what you're about to draw. It may also help you determine the best way to go about drawing something you have questions about or that appears challenging.

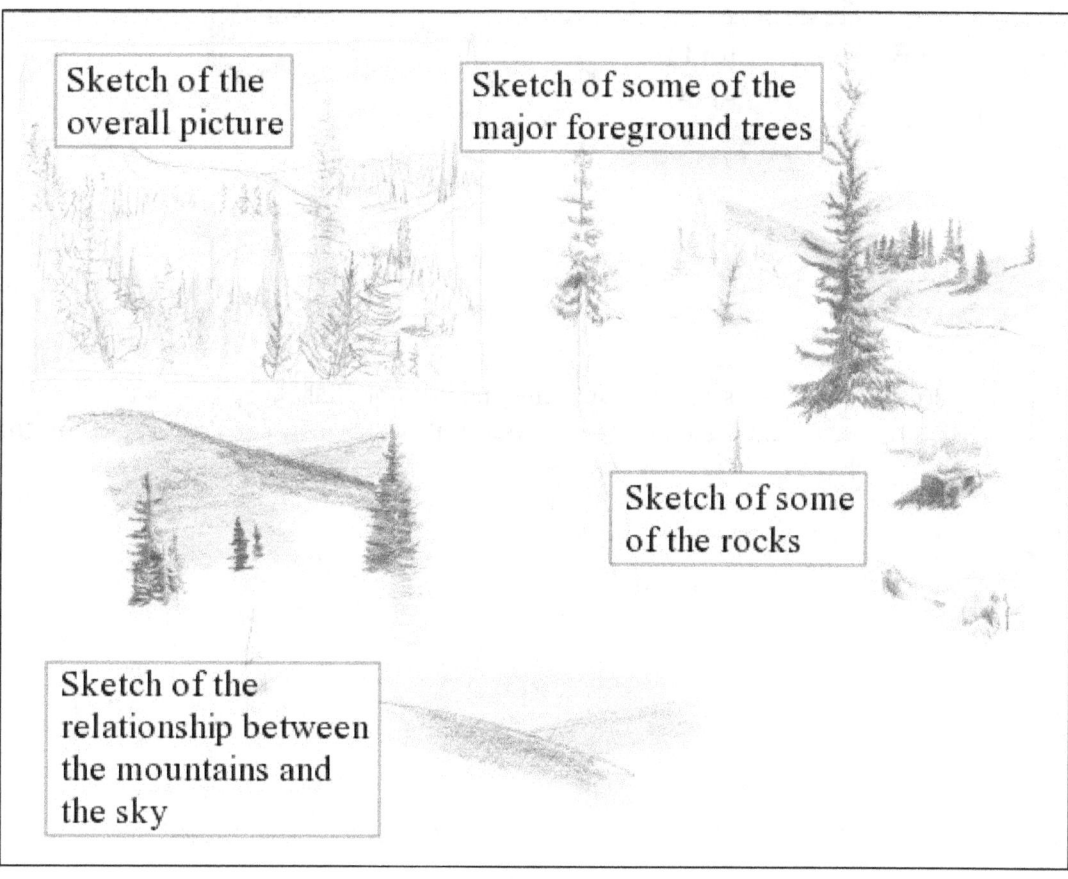

Figure 12-4. Studies and sketches for layout, shading, tone, tree and rock details

Step 3.

After you've studied the landscape through sketching, draw the initial layout of the major landmasses; in this case the mountains and small valley. The valley has a stream running through it which is shown by a diagonal line. The mountains are drawn so that the right one is behind the left.

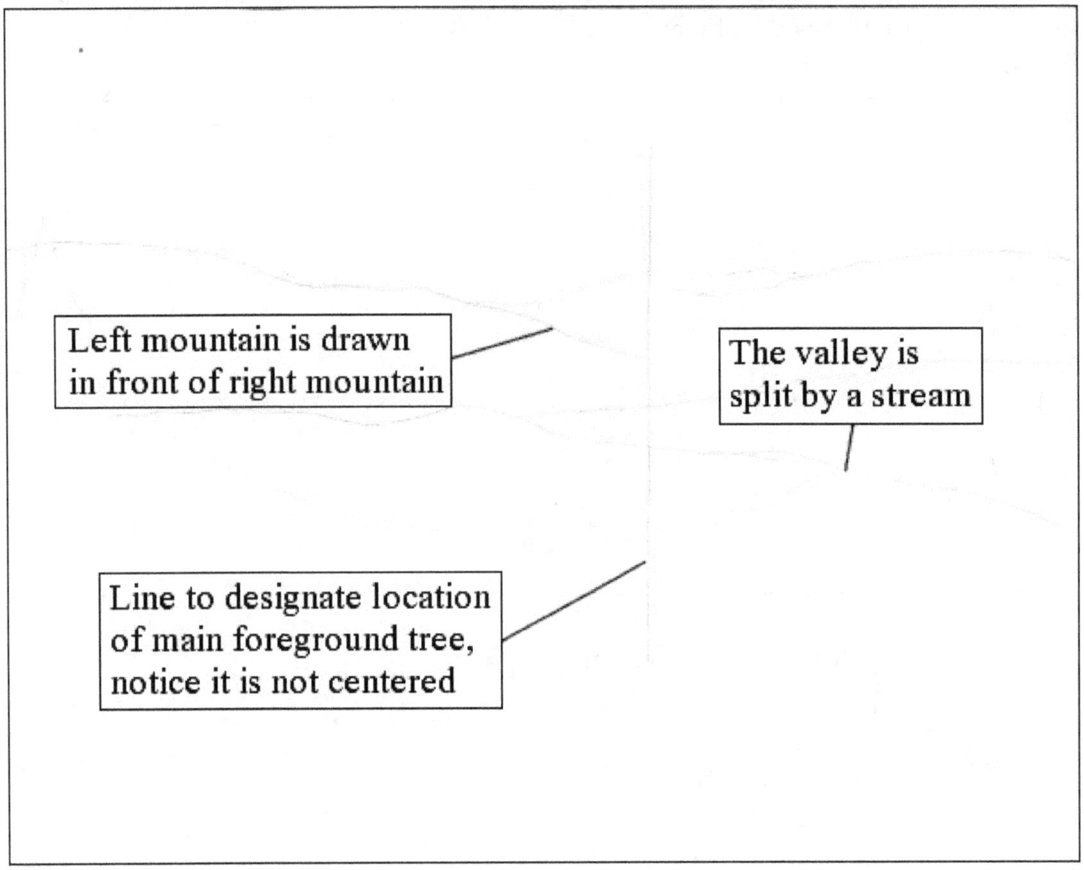

A line for the largest foreground tree is added. This line is used as a reference to tie all the other pieces together because the mountains converge and the stream runs out of site just to the left of this tree.

Notice that the main tree is offset to the right of center and that none of the mountains converge in the center. Also notice that there's more earth than sky and that the main tree goes a little over half way into the skyline.

Left mountain is drawn in front of right mountain

The valley is split by a stream

Line to designate location of main foreground tree, notice it is not centered

Figure 12-5. Initial layout of mountains, ground and main tree

This layout creates balance, stability, and will hopefully keep the viewer's eyes on the drawing. Before you move on to the next step make sure the layout is balanced keeping in mind all the layout tips mentioned before and in Volume 6.

After you've outlined the major landmasses, continue developing the scene by lightly sketching some of the main features. In the example below, the outlines of many of the major trees were added. These trees are the ones which are most noticeable in the picture. They were placed based on their relationship to the mountains, the main tree, and the far side of the valley.

At this point you only need to start locating features. Notice that the outlines of the trees below are very rough; most were made using hatch marks to locate the tips of the branches.

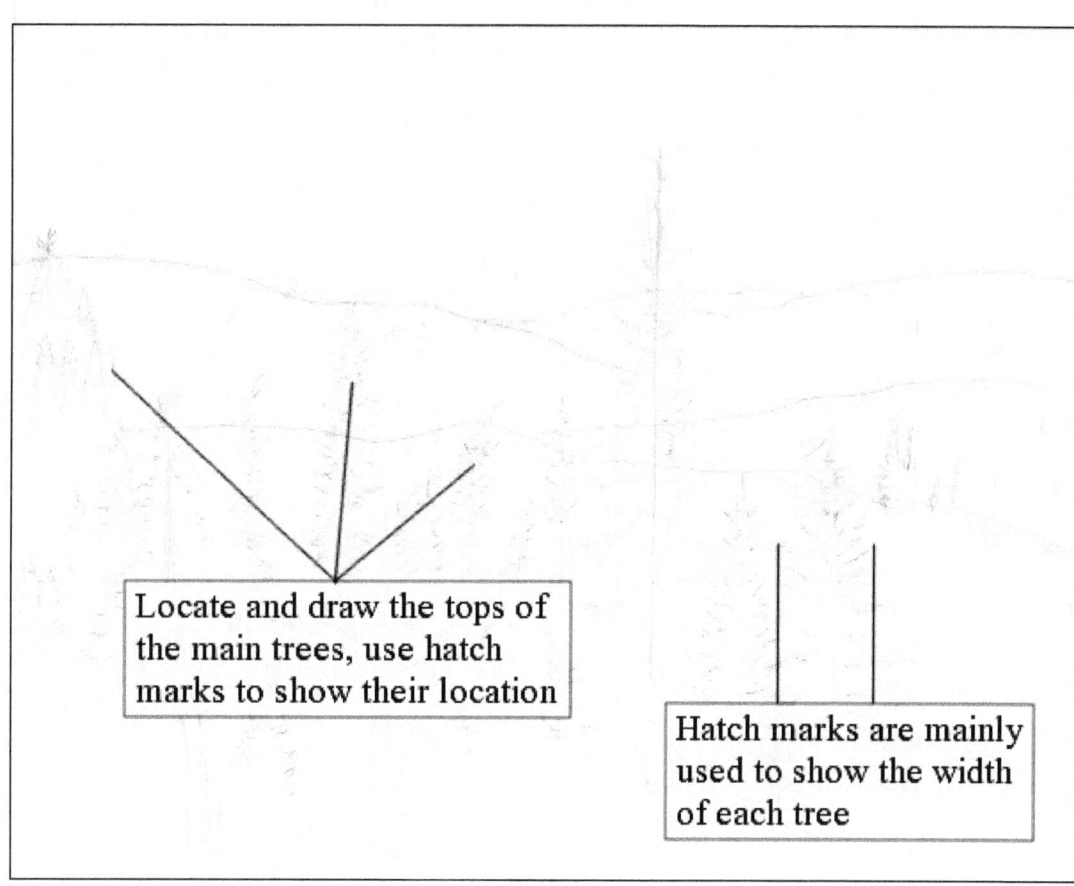

Figure 12-6. Layout of major treetops

31

Step 5.

Begin adding tone to the background, in this case the mountains and sky. Don't make the tone too dark yet unless you know that nothing with a lighter tone will be drawn over it. Notice below that the tone is kept light especially around the areas where the foreground trees will be drawn and where there are no trees on the mountain. Blend the tone to a uniform shade for each mountain and the sky.

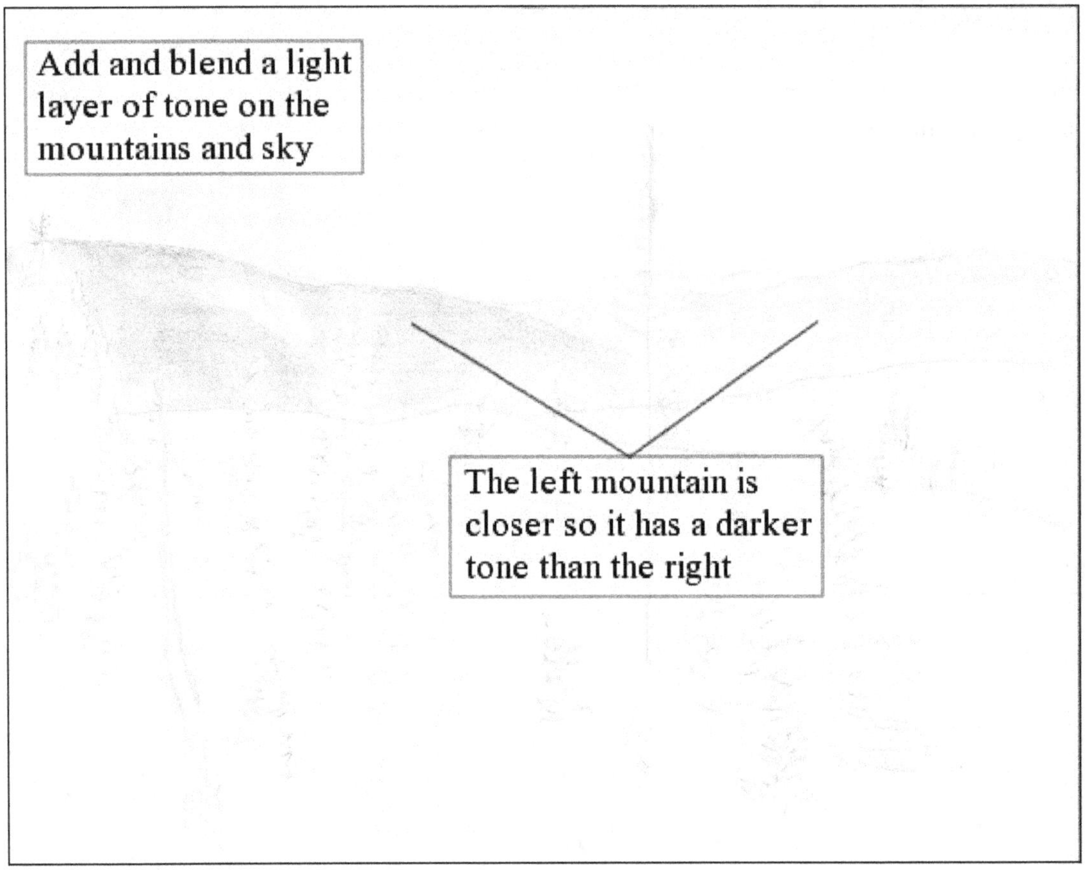

The tone of the mountain depends on how close it is to the viewer. As the mountains get further away from the viewer the color and tone get lighter. This happens because dust particles in the air block some of the light from reaching the eye. This is true of any object; the farther away it is the more particles there are between the viewer and object and the less detail and color will be seen.

Add and blend a light layer of tone on the mountains and sky

The left mountain is closer so it has a darker tone than the right

Figure 12-7. Tone added to the mountains and sky

Step 6.

At the far side of the valley there's a line of trees which effectively separates the foreground and background. Begin adding the trees along the edge of the valley. Use some of the larger trees as reference points to keep the layout accurate.

These trees are easy to draw. Using a tight grip, make small tight squiggles back and forth down the paper, from the top of the tree to the ground line. If you want to add more detail use two sets of squiggly lines, the one on the left a little darker than the one on the right. Drawing the trees with two sets of lines will do two things; it will make the right side of the tree appear to be highlighted, and it will separate the trees from each other so they don't look like a single block of tone.

As the line of background trees reaches the outlines of the foreground trees, increase the detail of the foreground tree outlines to reserve the space for when the time comes to detail them.

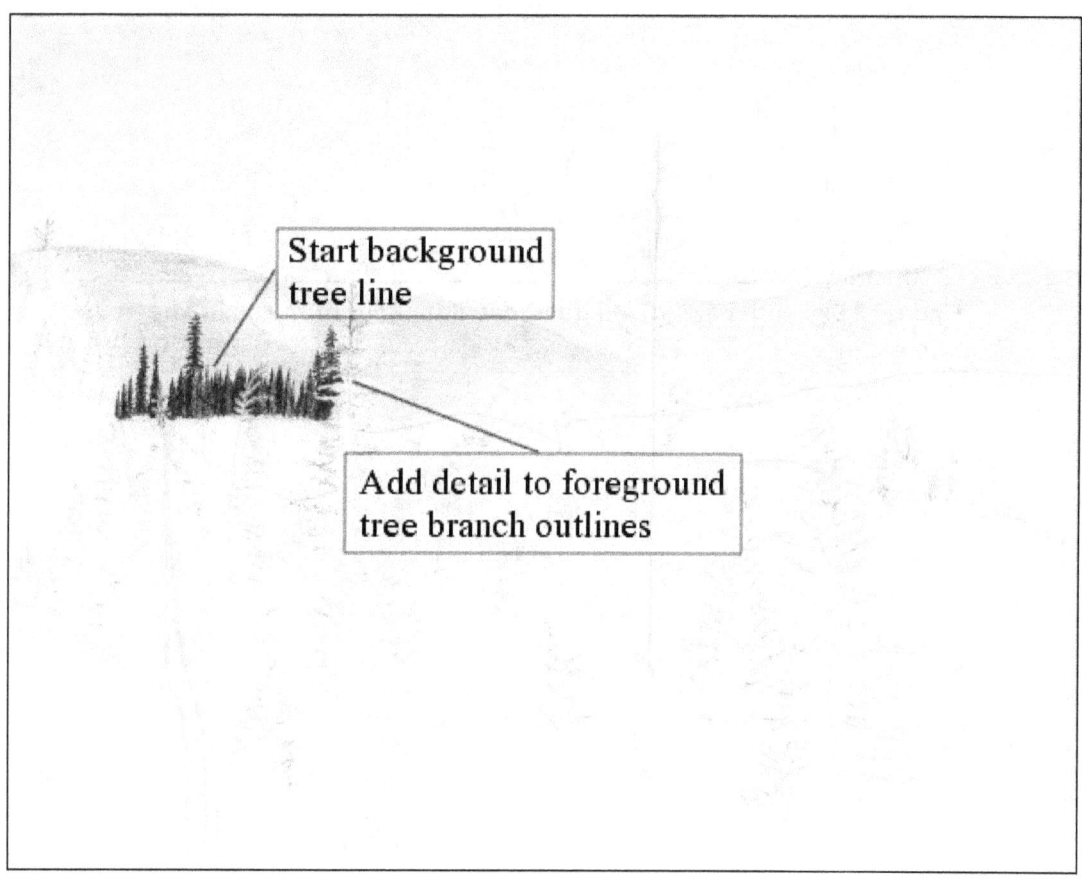

Figure 12-8. Start drawing background trees

Step 7.

Finish the background tree line and continue detailing the outline of the branches of the foreground trees.

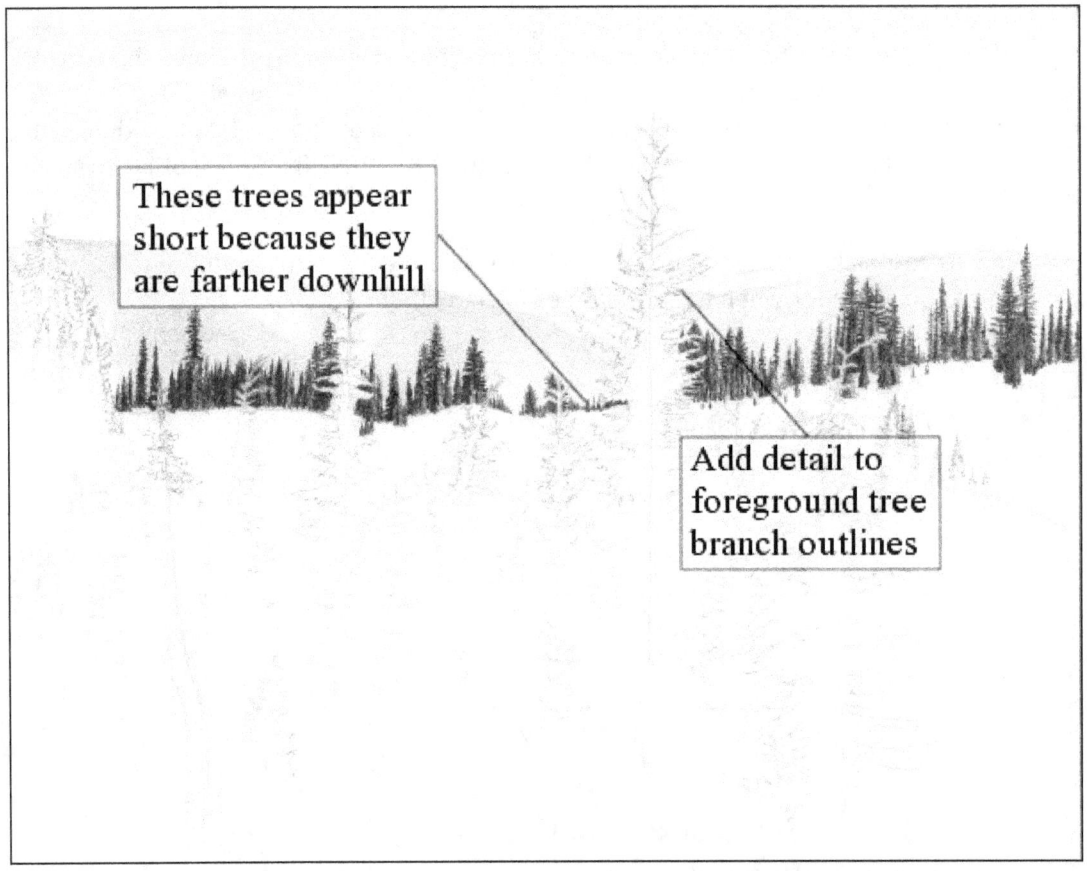

These trees appear short because they are farther downhill

Add detail to foreground tree branch outlines

Figure 12-9. Finish background trees, detail the tops of the main foreground tree outlines

With the background tree line finished it becomes easier to continue adding tone and detail to the mountains and sky.

Mountains have contours which can be shown with shading or hatching whenever a part of it slopes away from the sun. Shading and hatching were both used below to help create the contours in the mountains. Shading was used for a base layer of tone, then, tiny hatch marks were used to deepen the tone along the contours and give the mountain texture.

The mountain on the left is darker than the mountains on the right. It also has the largest highlighted area because of the space with no trees. The tone was blended lightly so that the texture of the hatch marks and paper would still be seen.

The mountains on the right are lighter and less detailed than the one on the left because they're further away.

Blend another layer of tone for the sky. In the example below, the left side of the sky doesn't have any clouds in it so it will be darker than the right side of the sky where the clouds are thin and bright white.

Add a base layer of tone to the areas connecting the background and foreground. In this case the valley was given some tone to connect the background trees to the foreground trees.

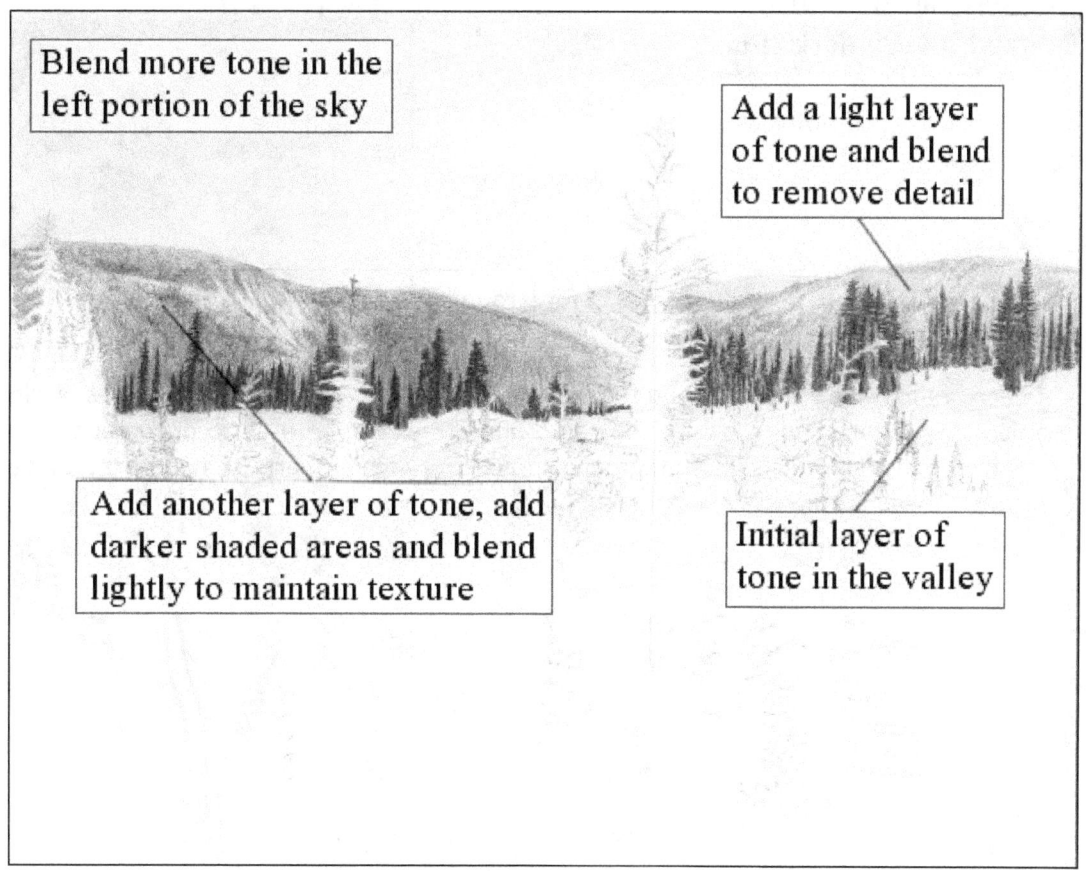

Figure 12-10. Deepen background tone, add texture

Step 9.

Begin adding tone to the foreground. In the case of the trees below this can take some time because of all the branches. In the photograph you can see that the trees have two shades of green, dark green where the tree is shaded and light green where the sun light hits it directly. A dark tone and a light tone are used to represent the two shades of green. The lighter tone is generally on the right side, the tops of branches, and occasionally on the tips of the left side branches.

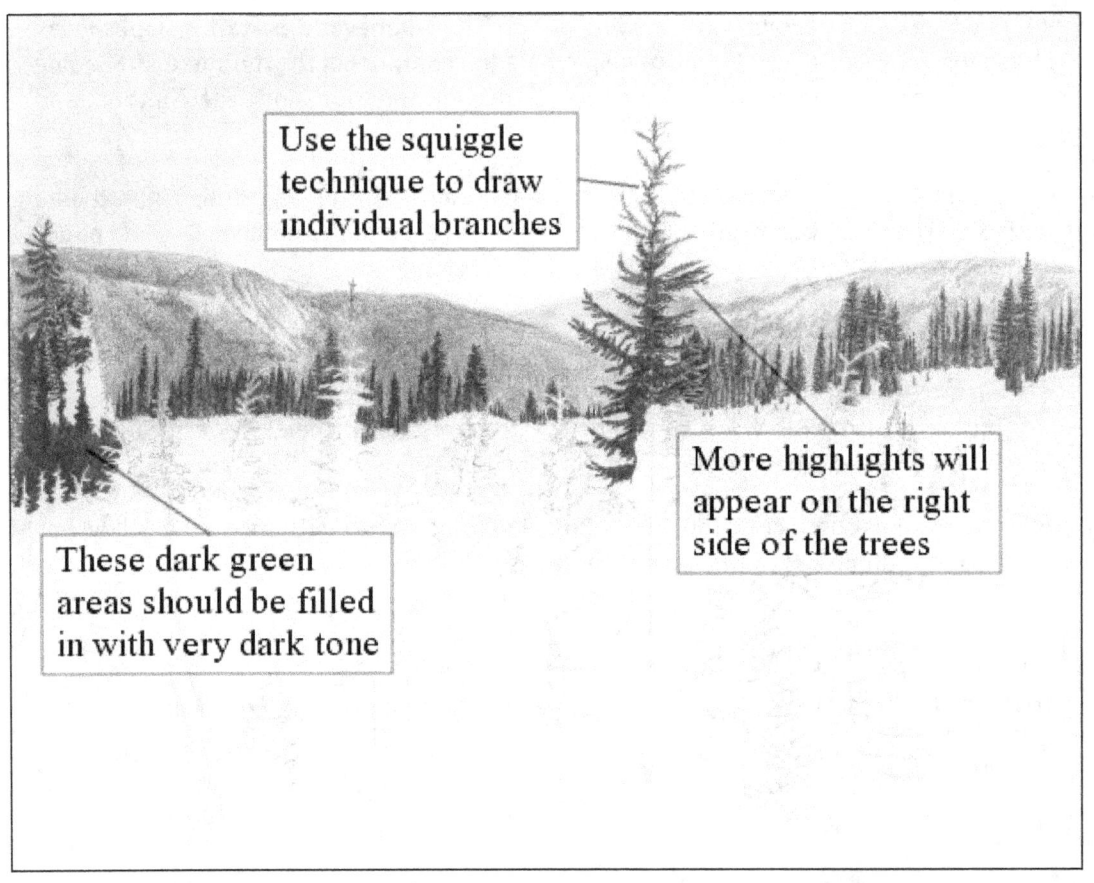

> Use the squiggle technique to draw individual branches

> More highlights will appear on the right side of the trees

> These dark green areas should be filled in with very dark tone

Figure 12-11. Start dark tones of foreground trees

Adding tone to the foreground can be done two ways, from lightest tone to darkest or darkest to lightest. In this example, dark blocks of tone were drawn in the areas where it was hard to tell one tree from another. For more distinct trees, the shaded side of each branch was drawn first and the lighter side second. For the main branches outlined earlier in Step 7, the same squiggle technique used for the background trees can be used to draw each individual branch. If you're concerned about drawing the foreground, practice sketching parts of it on a separate piece of paper before starting it on your drawing.

Continue detailing the foreground. Fill in individual branches of the major foreground trees that were outlined while drawing the background.

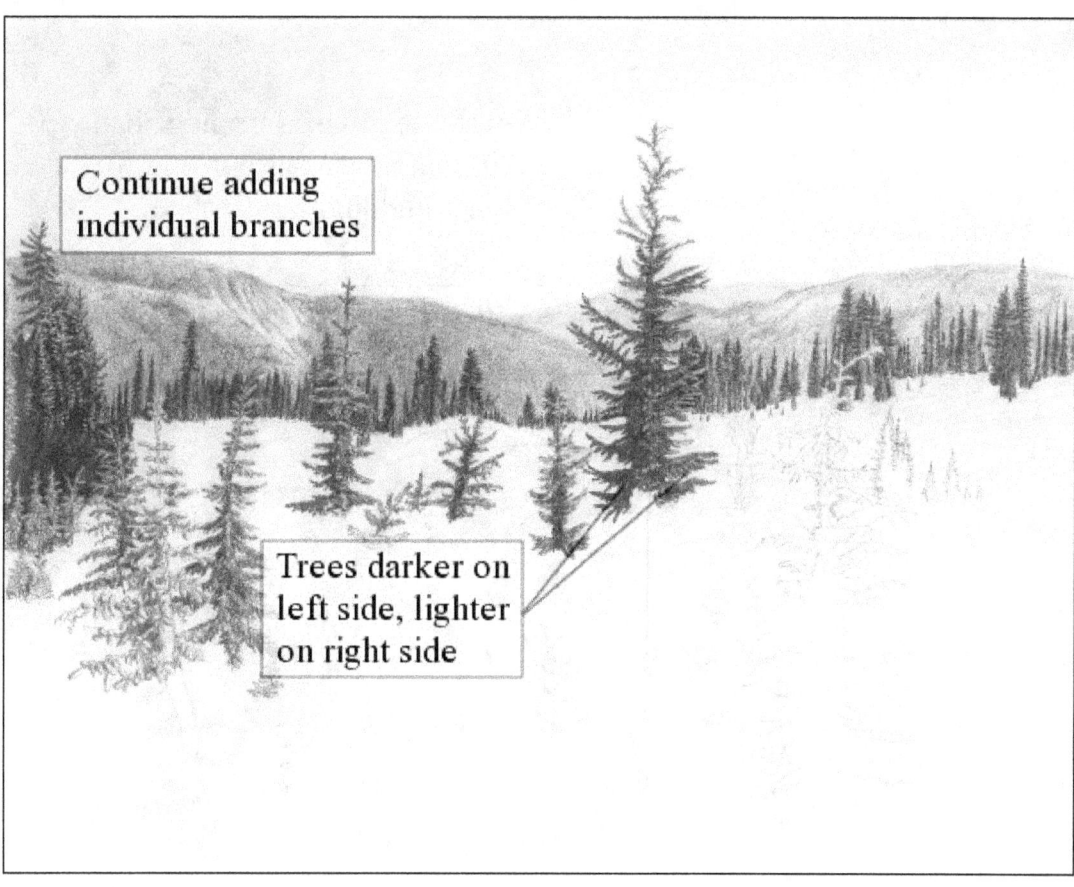

Figure 12-12. Foreground treetops

Step 11.

Once you've added tone in all the areas where the foreground crosses the background, evaluate your progress, adjust tones as needed, and plan a strategy to complete the foreground.

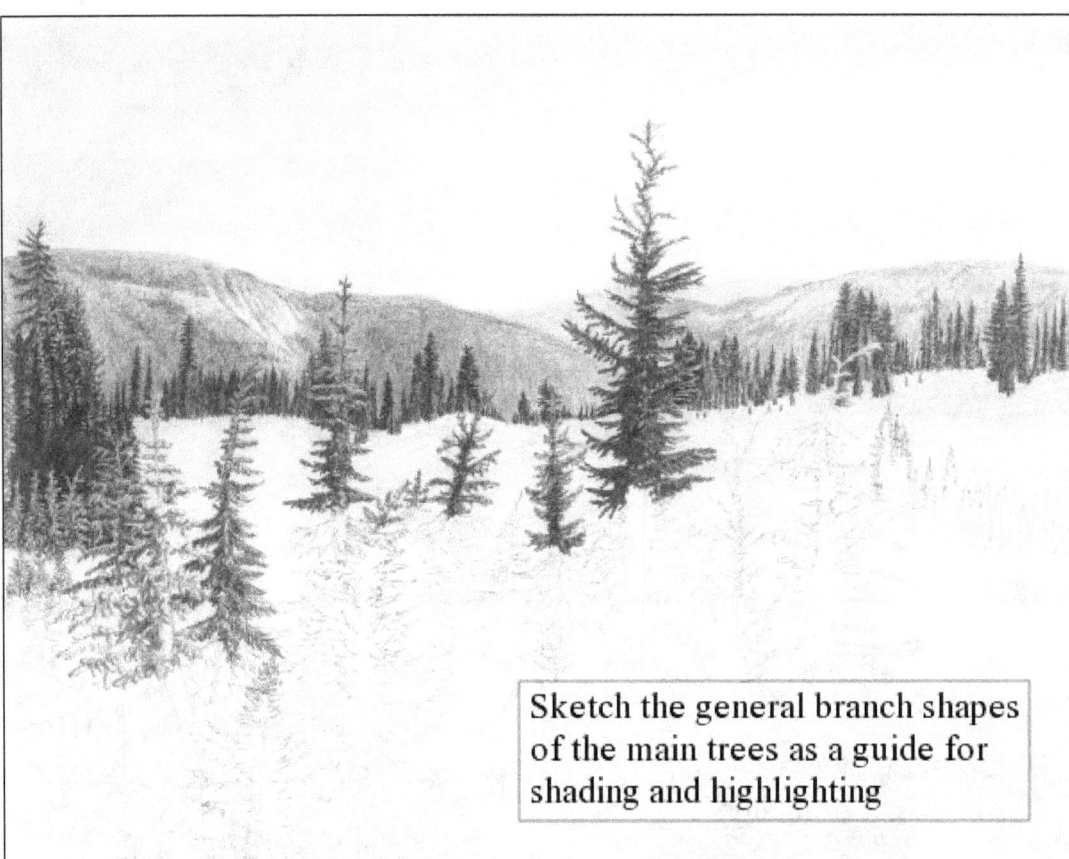

In this example, the rest of the major foreground tree branches were first outlined. These branches were sketched quickly, with just enough detail to guide the placement of shadows and highlights.

Sketch the general branch shapes of the main trees as a guide for shading and highlighting

Figure 12-13. Outline the remainder of the main foreground trees

With the foreground outlined you're ready to start detailing. Depending on the objects and the level of detail you intend to include this can take some time. Objects closer to the viewer will have more detail than objects in the background.

In the picture below, the branch outlines are used as guides to fill in the darkest areas of the trees which again are the bottom of each branch and the left side of each tree. The process of adding detail to the branches is what requires the most time on this particular drawing.

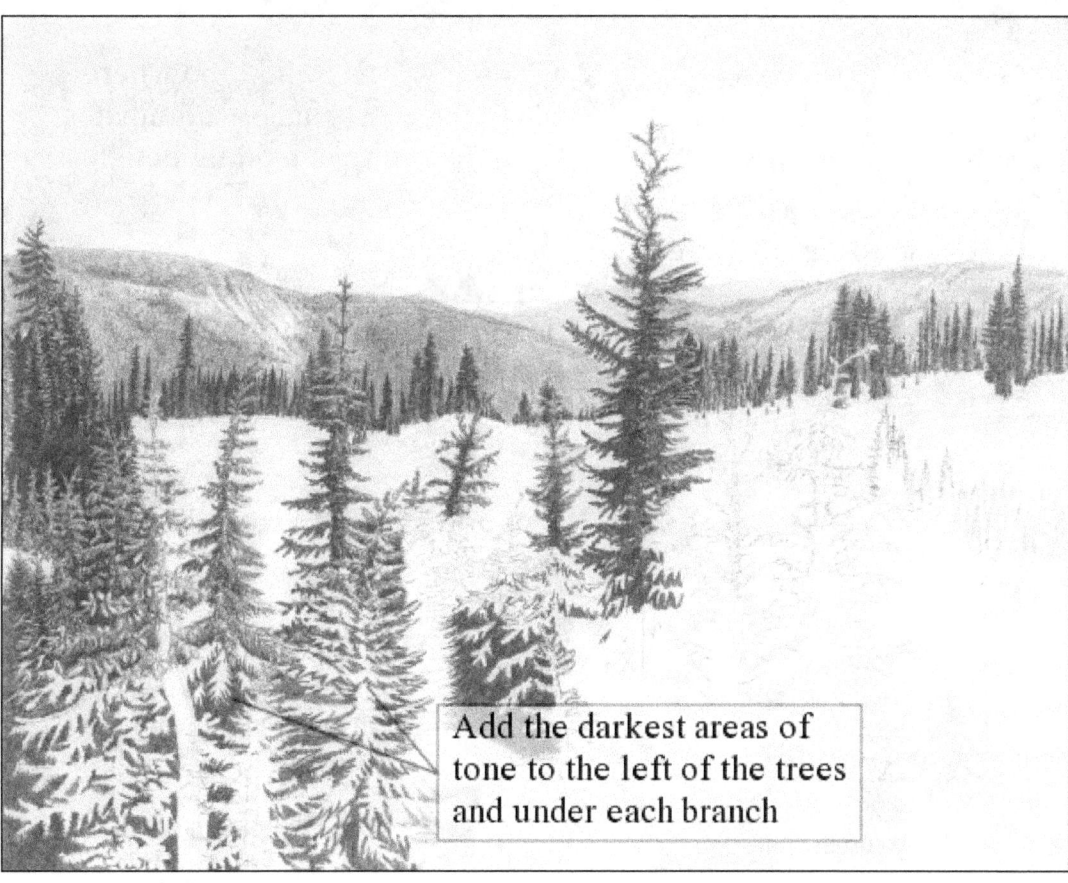

Add the darkest areas of tone to the left of the trees and under each branch

Figure 12-14. Develop dark tones in foreground trees

Step 13.

Finish adding the darkest tones.

In the picture below, all the major shaded areas have been added.

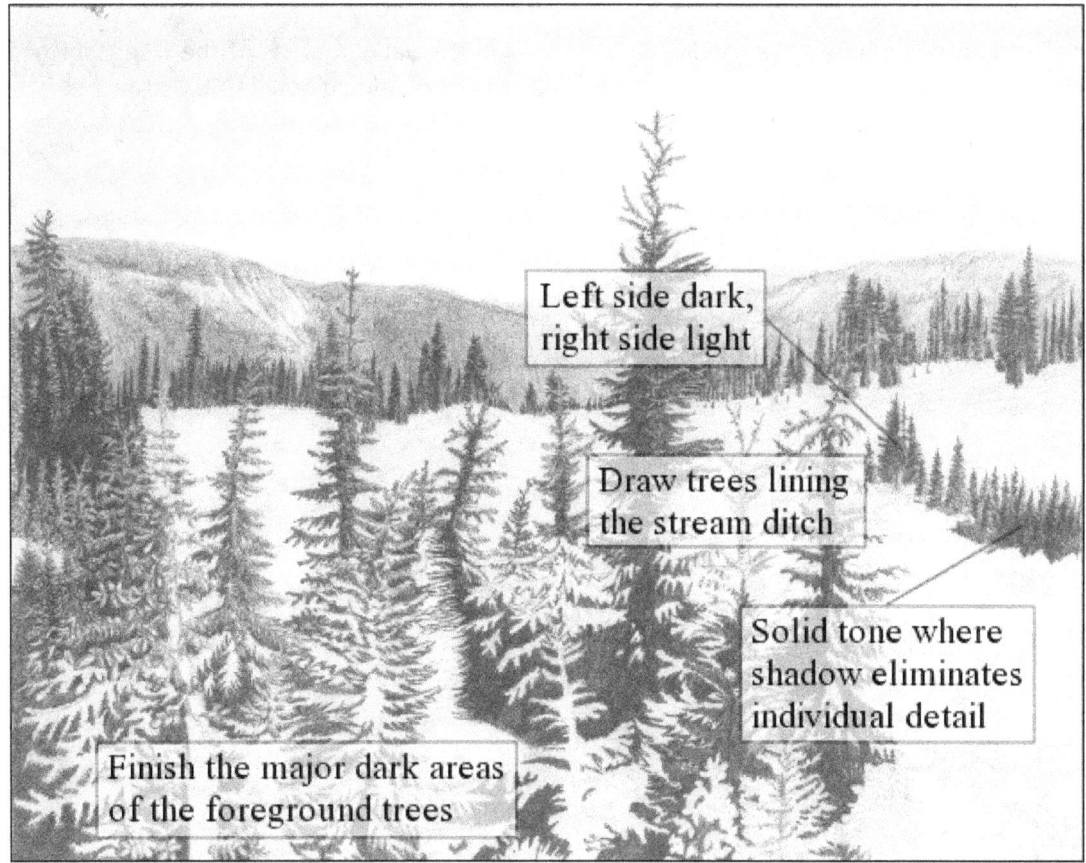

Left side dark, right side light

Draw trees lining the stream ditch

Solid tone where shadow eliminates individual detail

Finish the major dark areas of the foreground trees

Figure 12-15. Major dark tones in foreground trees finished

The group of trees lining the stream ditch was drawn using a technique similar to the one used for the trees in the background. Because the trees along the stream bank are closer to the viewer, it's more apparent that the left of each tree is darker than the right. Where these trees overlap and their colors are basically the same, they can be combined into a single block of tone.

With the darkest areas of tone complete, begin adding the lighter tones to complement them. If on the other hand you started with the light tones, begin working into the areas of darker tone.

For the trees in this example, adding the lighter layer of tone can be done a few different ways. You can use many small individual lines drawn in the general direction of the branches and needles, you can use small solid blocks of tone, or you can smudge the dark areas into the blank areas (if you're trying to achieve a sharp contrast between the two tones then smudging isn't recommended).

The drawing below was done using the first technique which is basically hatching (see Volume 3). If you're unsure about which technique to use, test each one on a separate sheet of paper to see which one you like best.

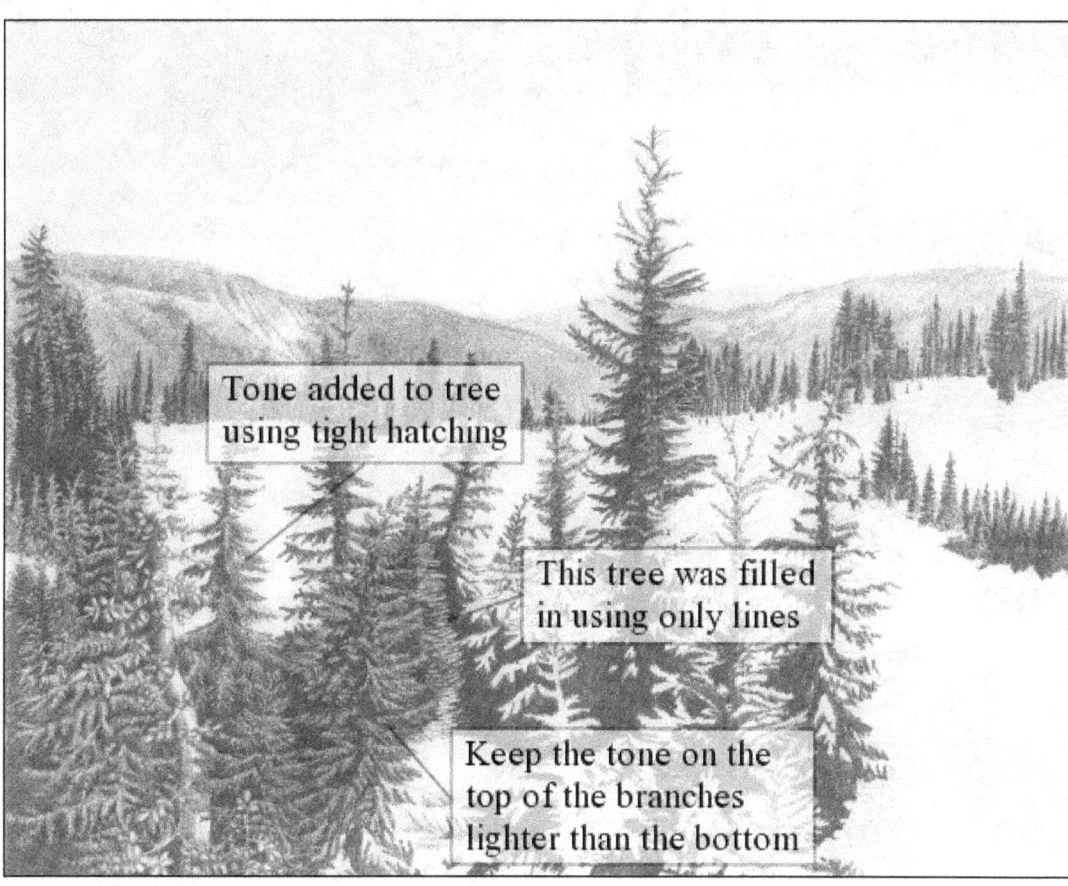

Figure 12-16. Develop light tones and highlights in foreground trees

Step 15.

Continue adding the lighter tones and highlights. At the same time, adjust the shadows and darker tones to create good transitions between light and dark.

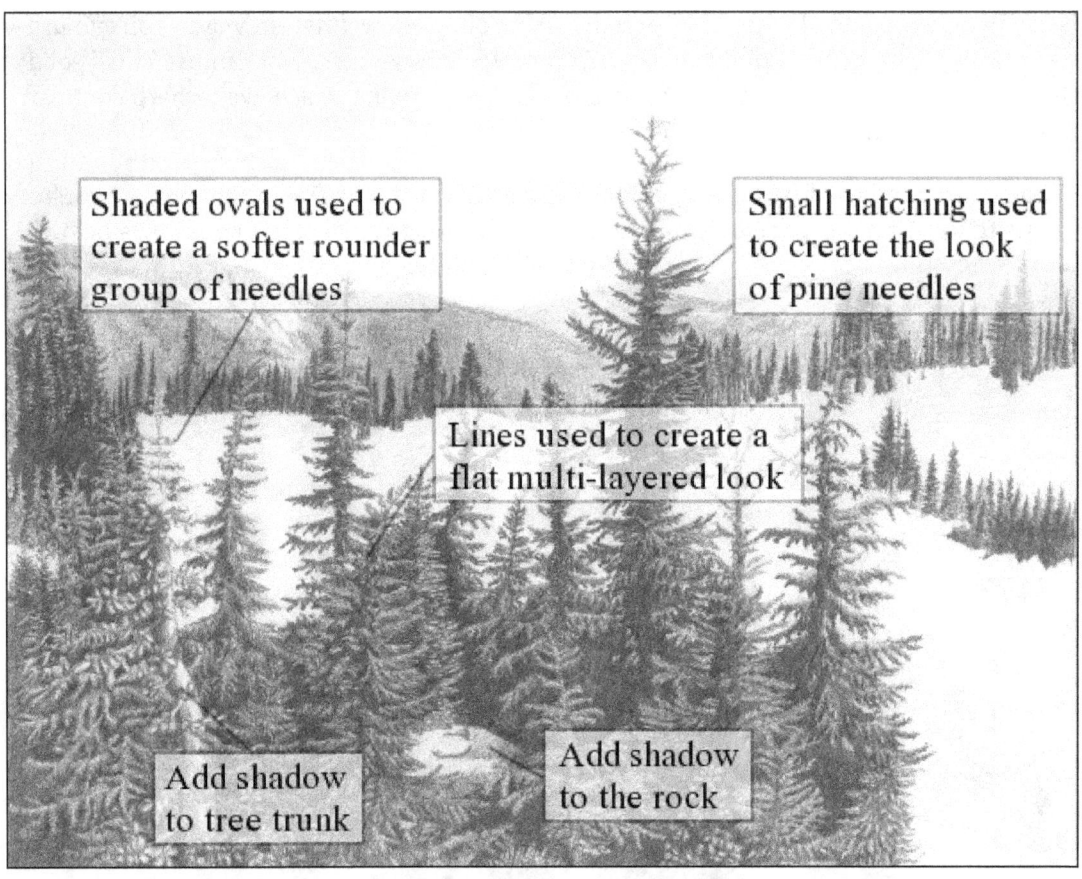

In this example, different techniques were used to finish the lighter tones depending on the type of tree and its features. It's not required to use the same technique for each tree; they're all a little different.

Figure 12-17. Complete lighter tones and highlights for foreground trees

With the foreground and the background done your drawing may be complete. Take another look at your drawing and determine if there's anything between the foreground and background that must be added to tie them together.

In the example below there's a large area in the field that needs to be filled to connect the foreground and background. There are groups of trees that need to be added behind the foreground trees, as well as small ridges and various rocks that need to be added in the valley.

Shadows from the trees in the background also need to be added. The shadows are important, they will finish the three dimensional effect of all the objects in the drawing. They'll also give the viewer clues as to the time of day and where the light source is.

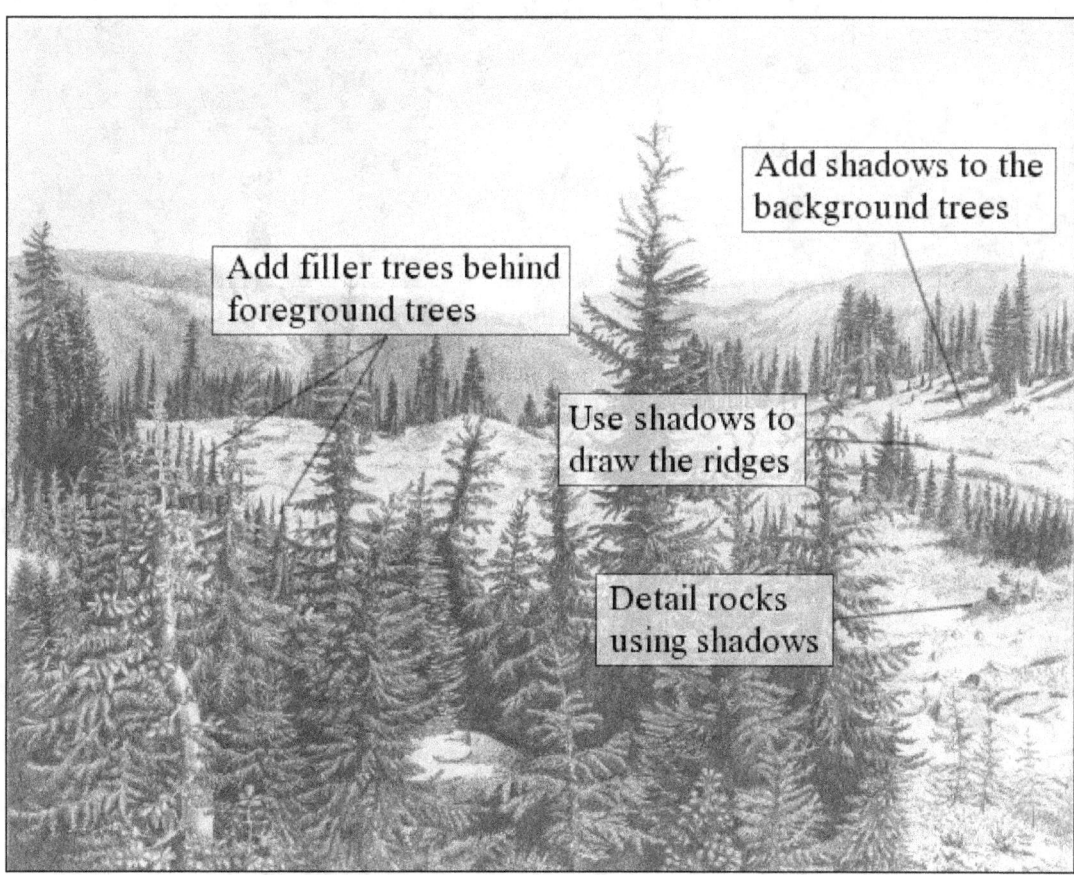

Figure 12-18. Add tone and shadows to the field

Step 17.

Start tying everything together as you begin applying the finishing touches. Blend the tone of the background and adjust the tones of the foreground to create a smooth transition between the two areas.

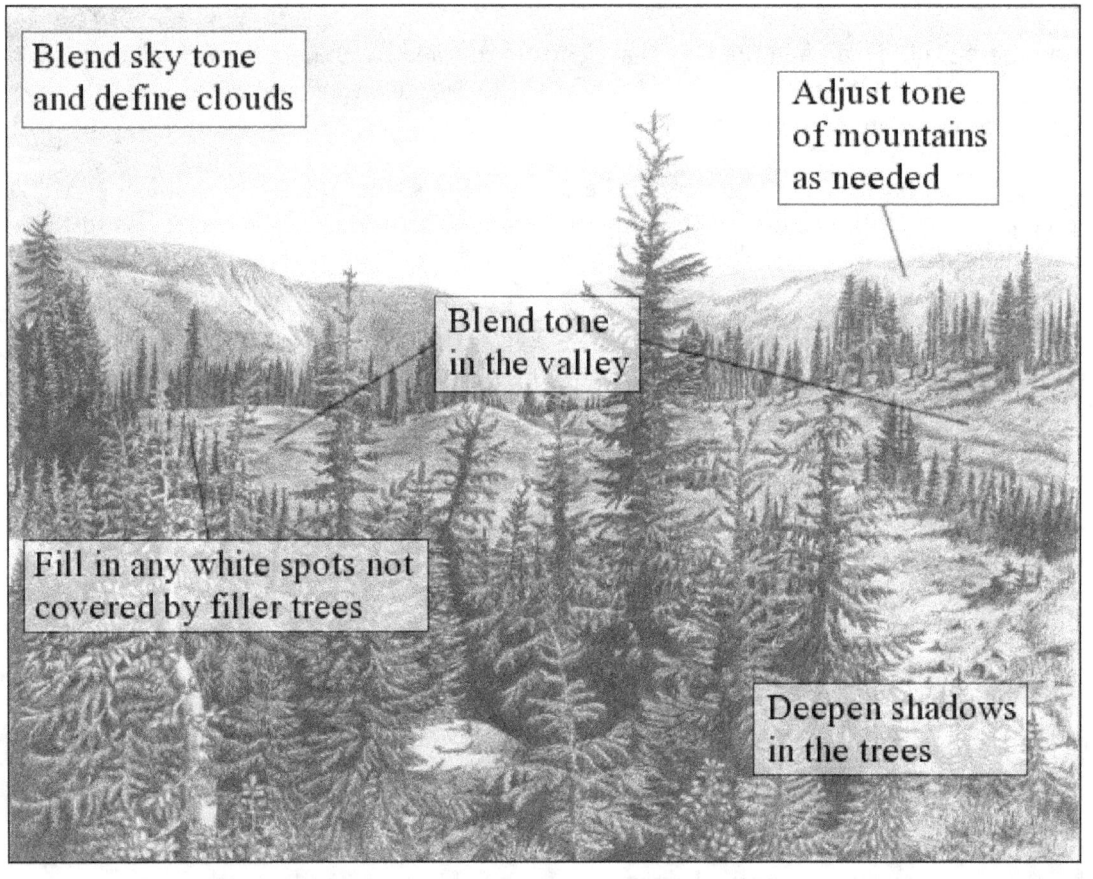

Fill gaps that are still untouched. Typically this can be done with random foliage or rocks; it doesn't have to be specific or detailed.

Check the tone of the sky and clouds. Use an eraser to clean up the clouds and make them white.

Check the tone of the background; adjust it if necessary to appear less defined and further away.

Deepen the tone and shadows of the foreground.

Figure 12-19. Deepen tone and shadow in the valley, clean up sky

Continue from Step 17 improving the finishing touches. This process can actually take a considerable amount of time. Typically if you look long enough at your drawing compared to the photograph you'll see differences and be able to correct or improve them. The time spent finishing a drawing such as this really depends on the amount of detail you're trying to achieve.

The most significant change below is in the tone of the valley and the sky. Some adjustments were made to the trees of the foreground but considering how dense the foliage in this area is; adding more detail to the foreground is basically unnoticeable.

One thing that hasn't been focused on much in this process is the highlights. Most plants in a large landscape like this aren't extremely reflective but you still need to be aware of the brightest areas and make sure to include these as they're still important for creating a full three dimensional look. Check rocks, water, the tips of branches, exposed tree trunks and large leaves (especially if they're wet) as these are the most likely places you'll find definite highlights.

Continue adding detail and adjusting until you're satisfied.

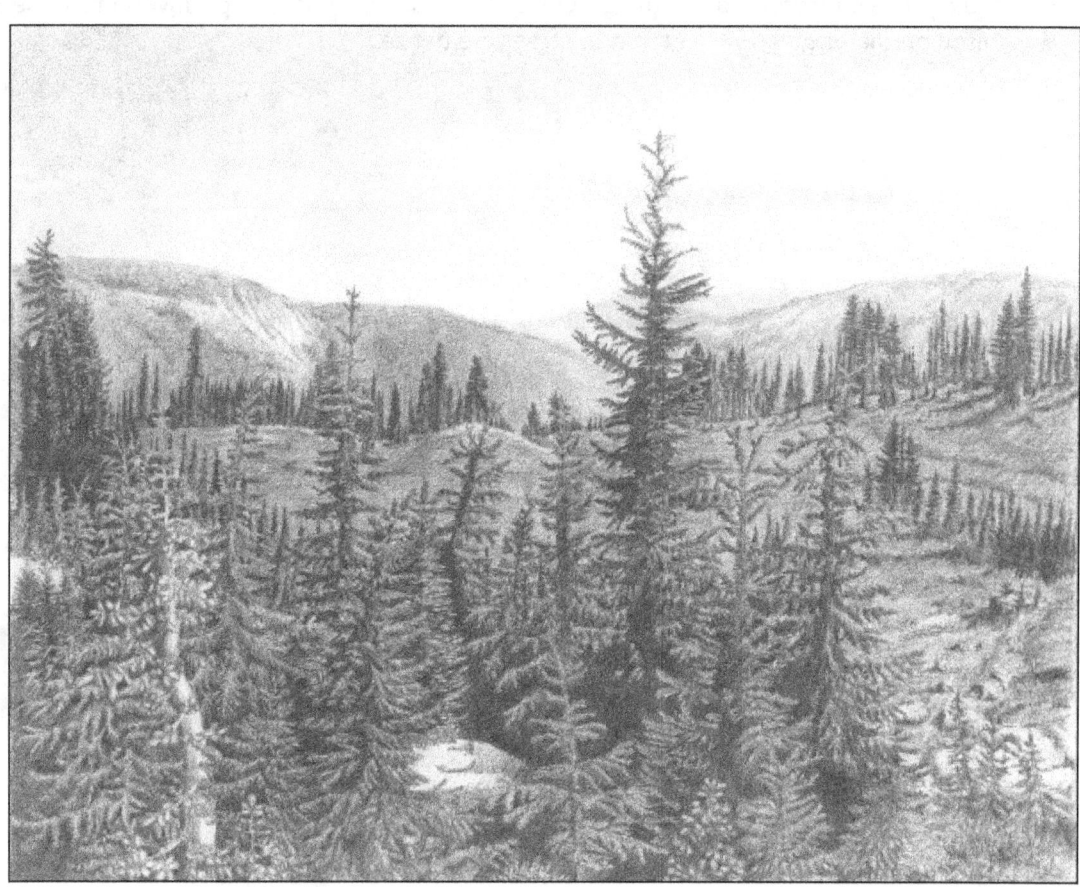

Figure 12-20. Finishing touches added

Results and Comparisons

Once again it's good practice to compare your drawing side by side with the picture to find differences.

The most noticeable difference between the drawing and photograph is that the photograph is much darker than the drawing. Like the still life drawing in Volume 11, part of the reason for the difference in tone is the conversion from paper to a digital image, also the fact that a No. 2 pencil was used rather than a softer one like a 6B.

Another reason why the drawing is not as dark as the photo is that a piece of folded paper was used for blending. Paper is harder and stiffer than tissue or a tortillon and if you push too hard as you're blending you can scratch the surface of the drawing, so the blending and smudging in this example was done lightly. The result is that very small white areas are still left in the paper which makes the drawing look lighter.

The trees in the drawing are not exactly the same as the ones in the photograph but that's okay. The branches of the groups of trees in the photograph are so complex that in order to get them exactly the same you would have to either trace them or project the picture onto your paper and draw them. Tracing all the branches and trying to match each one exactly would be very time consuming, there'd be little extra benefit from the time put into it. The interpretation of the groups of trees is close enough for anyone to understand that the drawing was based on the photograph and that the trees are dense.

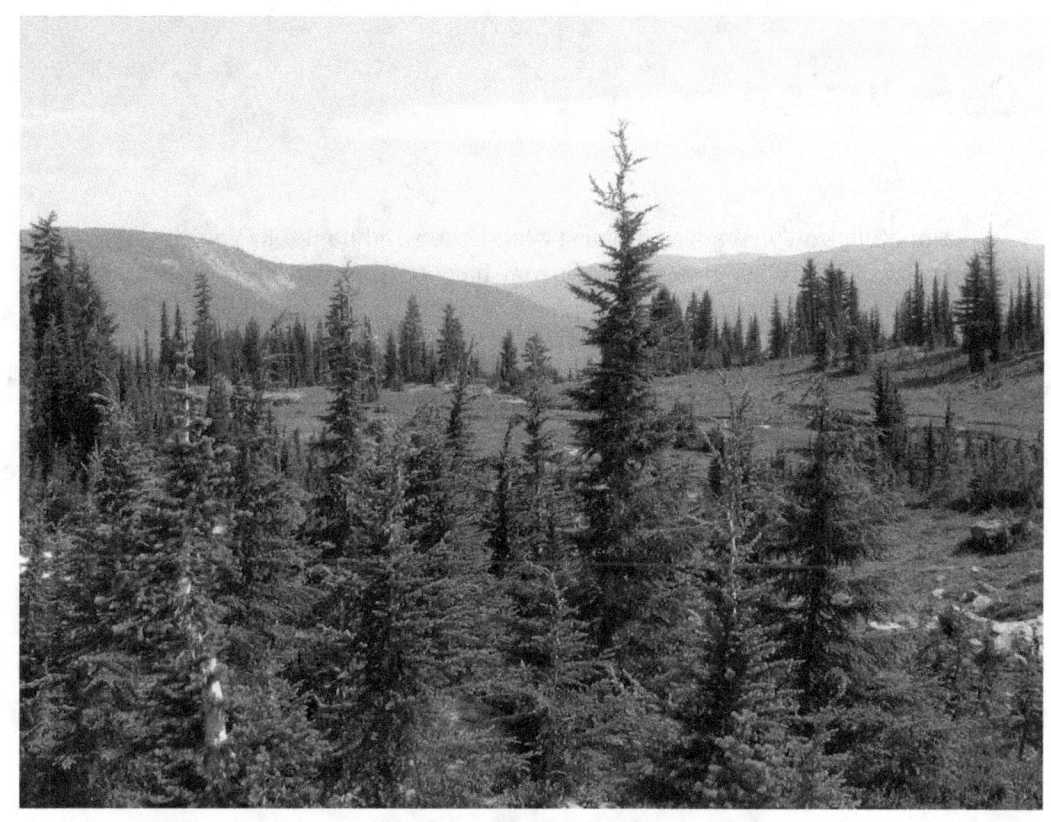
Figure 12-21. Mountain forest landscape photograph

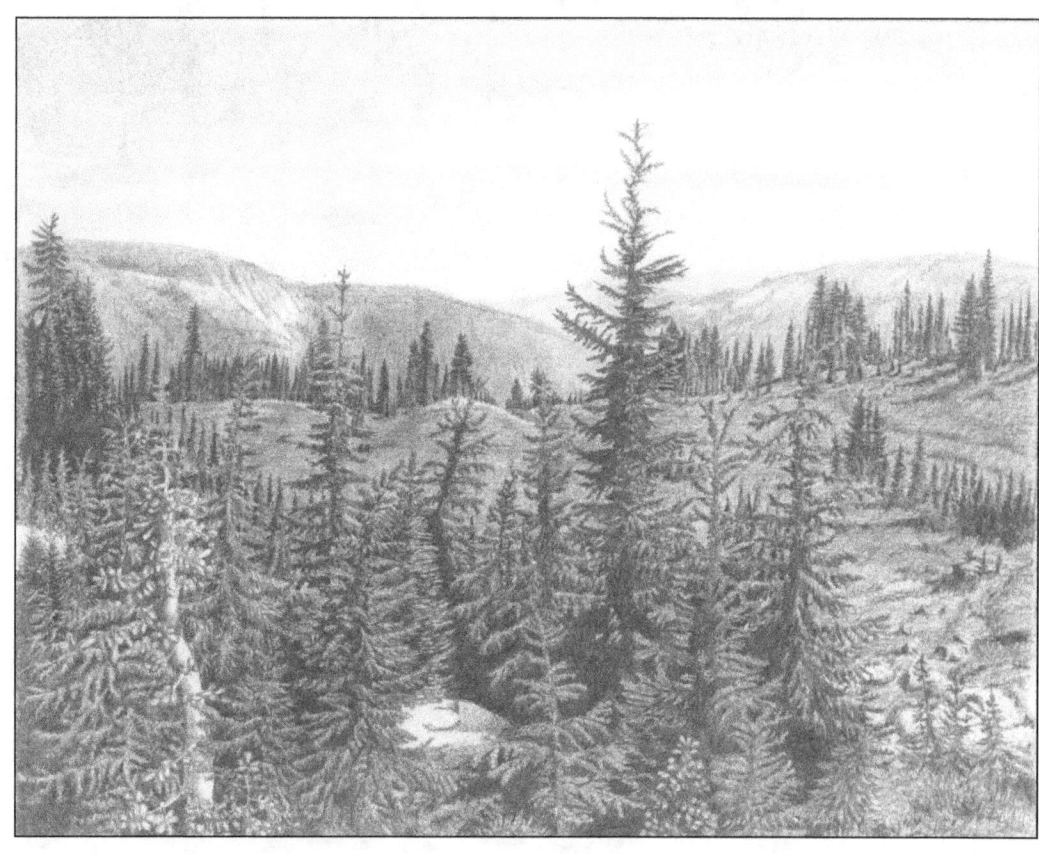
Figure 12-22. Completed landscape drawing

Conclusion

Hopefully you've enjoyed drawing a landscape and hopefully you've learned some principles that you can apply to future landscape drawings. You may have noticed that none of the examples in this lesson contained a building or man-made structure, next time you draw a landscape try including one.

When including a man-made structure make sure to find the vanishing points and use perspective lines to help guide the layout (see Volumes 3 and 10).

When you start your next landscape, remember the layout tips from this lesson regarding balance and keeping the viewer's eyes on the drawing.

And finally, enjoy learning about nature and the world we live in as you draw the landscapes around you.

Portrait Drawing

Welcome to Volume 13. The purpose of this lesson is to introduce you to portrait drawing and give you a tool you can use to create accurate drawings of people's faces. It won't cover everything about drawing faces, there's simply too much information for one lesson, but it will give you some basic principles to follow and a tool to use.

This lesson together with Volume 9 on sketching people and animals will give you a solid foundation of knowledge and basic skills which you'll be able to build on. Developing these skills is something that will take time and practice.

What is a Portrait?

A portrait is an artistic representation of a person with the focus typically being on the face. It's okay to include more of the body and even the entire person but traditionally a portrait includes the head to just below the shoulders.

Portraits have been around for thousands of years but the reason for drawing them has continually changed.

Ancient Egyptians carved and painted profile portraits of their kings and leaders to document history. The ancient Greeks painted realistic three quarter and full frontal view portraits of family members who had passed away. These paintings would then be buried along with the relative.

Throughout Europe portraits were painted to document the history of rulers as well as the conditions of regular people. They were also used as keepsakes for loved ones and marriage proposal cards.

Even after the invention of the camera portraits have maintained a valuable place in our culture and people still buy them but the reason has once again changed.

We no longer need portraits to document history; photographs are faster and more effective for that. But people continue to buy portraits for family keepsakes, the novelty, to stay current with pop culture, or because they enjoy the interpretation or emotion the artist was able to capture. There are many reasons why portraits are appealing; the point is that portrait art still has a strong place in society.

Different Styles

There've been three main approaches or styles of portraits.

The first style is realism, or drawing/painting exactly what's seen, to get as close a likeness as possible to the person modeling the portrait.

The second style is idealism, where the artist enhances the person's features or removes blemishes to make them look better or more attractive than they really are.

The last major style is abstract. In an abstract portrait the artist may distort or remove facial features, change their placement and/or use unnatural colors. This is done to create a certain feeling or emotion, or to just give an impression of the subject. This style is very exploratory.

These three styles have been mixed to various degrees throughout history. The style you choose is up to you as an artist.

The Benefits of Portrait Drawing

Portraits are fun to draw for several reasons. As you draw portraits and study the facial features and details of your model, you'll find you gain great insight into the person you're drawing. If you're drawing a person you know, you'll probably notice things about that person's face that you never saw before.

Another reason portraits are fun is because they're challenging. No two people are exactly the same even though in general everyone has the same features. The slight variations in proportions and shapes are what make everyone unique. Finding and correctly drawing individual variations is the challenge.

Last of all, you'll receive a lot of satisfaction from sharing your ability and being able to give someone a portrait they can enjoy for the rest of their life.

Finding a Model

To get a model there are three things you can do.

First, you can find models from real life by asking people if they'll sit still while you draw them. This takes patience on the part of the model so make sure they're comfortable and entertained either by music, conversation, or something to watch or do while they sit. Generally it's easier to use adults for this; they're typically more patient than kids. It's hard for young children to sit still for long periods of time. The advantage to this method is that the subject is right in front of you in 3-D, you can walk around them and study their features from different angles before beginning and while drawing them. You may also have the ability to try different lighting.

You don't necessarily have to set up a pose. If you see someone doing a task, you can draw them right there. Be aware that they'll probably move and may even leave so if you're going to draw this way you'll need to develop a bit of speed.

The second place to find a model is from a photograph. This method is very convenient and has some unique advantages. First, you can take the picture with you and work on the portrait at any time, wherever you are, and you won't have to worry about asking or scheduling time to sit with them. Second, you can capture a moment of emotion. It takes a lot of energy for a model to display extreme emotions like happiness or sadness for long periods of time but a picture can capture the moment forever. Using pictures is a good way to draw children too. Third, you can draw people you've never met. The major disadvantage to using photographs is that you won't be able to change the view, angle or lighting, however with enough practice you can overcome these obstacles.

The last method is not to use a model at all, but just make someone up in your mind. Once you learn some basic principles about portraits and drawing different facial features, you can use that knowledge to draw faces however you want and to create people who don't really exist.

Views

There are three main views or head positions: full frontal, three quarter view, and profile.

Full frontal view is when the person is looking directly at you. These can be a little challenging for a beginner especially around the nose. In this view none of the features are at an angle so people tend to draw them very flat looking.

Three quarter view is when a person's head is looking to the left or right at roughly a 45 degree angle. This view is a little easier for a beginner to draw because it's easier to see how the shapes and dimensions of the face interact with each other. This typically helps the beginner create a drawing that looks more three dimensional.

A profile view is when the person's head is turned ninety degrees to you so you only see one side of their face. Most portraits aren't done in this view even though it's a relatively simple view to draw. Like the full frontal view there's a chance that portraits done in profile view will look a bit two dimensional if shading and highlights are not done correctly.

Facial features must be drawn differently in each view. For example, the eyes in a full frontal view will be shaped more or less like an almond and the pupil will be round, but when turned in profile the eye is shaped like a wide piece of pie and the pupil is skinny and slightly elliptical. A common mistake many beginners make is that they learn how to draw a facial feature in one view and then apply it to all the views. Good observation skills will help correct this but if you're drawing from your mind it'll be helpful to know how to draw each feature in each view.

Lighting

Lighting is something you need to consider. As you know, a face has many ins and outs, it's not flat but it's not exactly round like a ball either. The wrong lighting will create shadows that can distort features and change the mood of the portrait.

A traditional portrait will look best when there's a soft light source a little above and to the left or right of the model. This will create just enough shadow and highlight to show all the features without casting dark heavy shadows across the face.

If the intent is to depict a more extreme look then you can use lighting that creates more shadows. A stronger more direct light or a different light source location will change the depth and size of the shadows on the face.

Framing the Portrait

Framing refers to the placement of the portrait on the paper. It doesn't look good to position the head so that it's in the center of the paper. If the head is located in the center of the paper you may not have enough room for the neck and shoulders, the person will look like they're squatting down and the portrait won't be balanced.

Locate the head so the upper lip is just under the center of the paper. If drawing a three quarter or profile view, shift the location of the head a little to the left or right so there's slightly more room on the paper in the direction the eyes are looking.

A Portrait Tool

The drawing tool mentioned in the introduction is really a method for laying out the facial features with the correct proportions and positions; it's called the grid method. There are some initial limitations to using it but there are also some good advantages.

The limitations that come with using this method are that you have to have a photograph of the person you want to draw. In addition to that, you won't learn as much about drawing generic facial features as quickly.

The advantages to using the grid method are that you'll learn to judge relative distances and train your visual memory as you transfer a photograph to a piece of paper.

Once you learn this method the advantages will always be available to you and if you use it often the disadvantages decrease. As you consistently draw more people you'll start to get a feel for layout, shape, and tone of facial features. You'll develop your own techniques and styles for drawing the eyes, ears, nose and mouth and you'll be able to draw these features without the use of a photograph or grid. You'll gain an understanding of where the facial features should be in relation to each other and you'll eventually be able to draw people from your head or draw someone sitting in front of you.

Learn a few more basic layout principles in addition to the grid method and your ability to draw portraits will greatly increase. You are encouraged to read Volume 9 which has a more extensive section on general facial features and layout.

The first step of the grid method is to get a photograph of the person you want to draw. Make sure the face in the picture isn't too small. Below are some examples of good pictures to use. This lesson uses the picture in Figure 13-1, the picture in Figure 13-2 with the baby is also available for you to use. Babies are more challenging to draw than adults because their features are very soft and subtle.

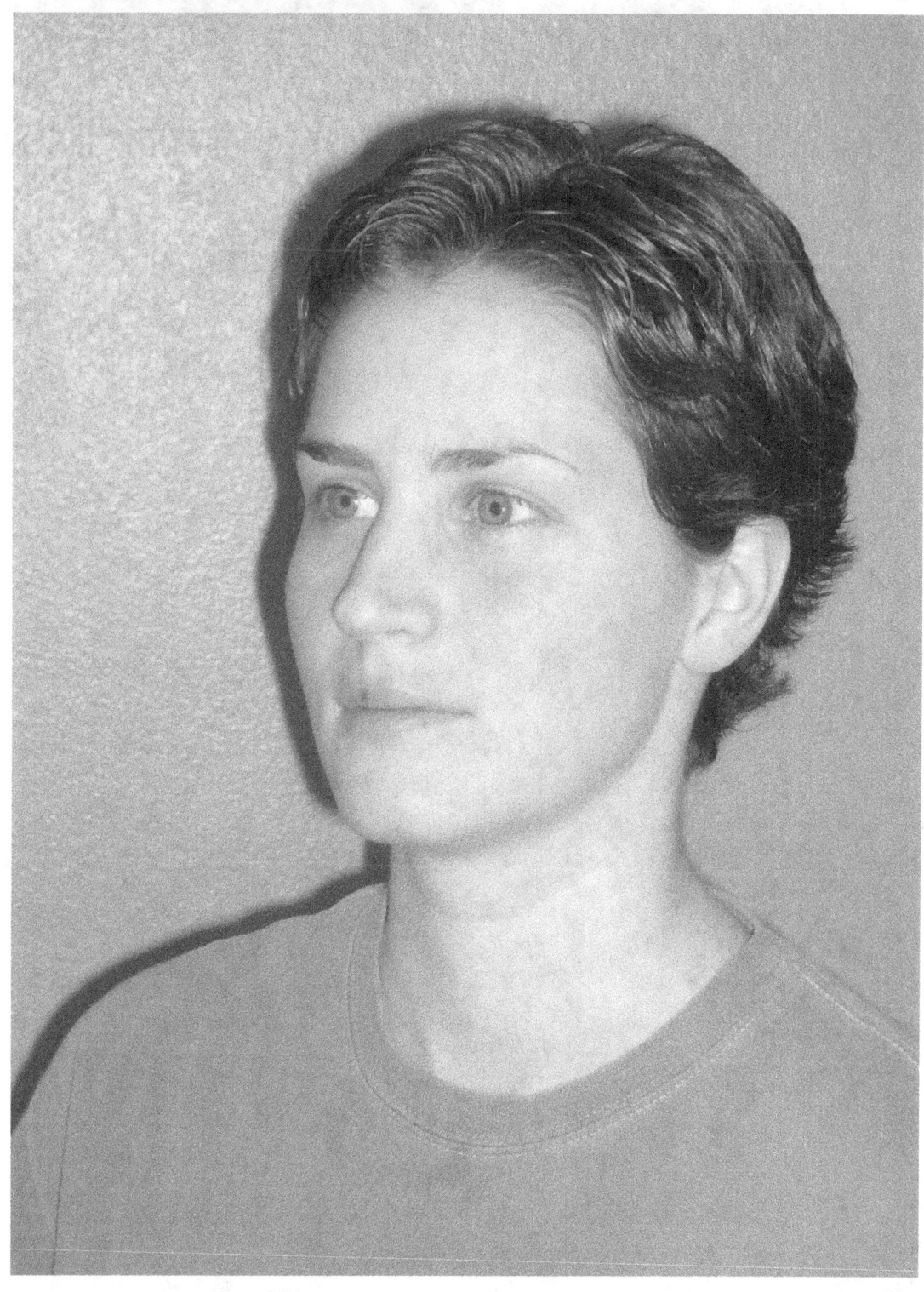

Figure 13-1. Woman in three quarter view

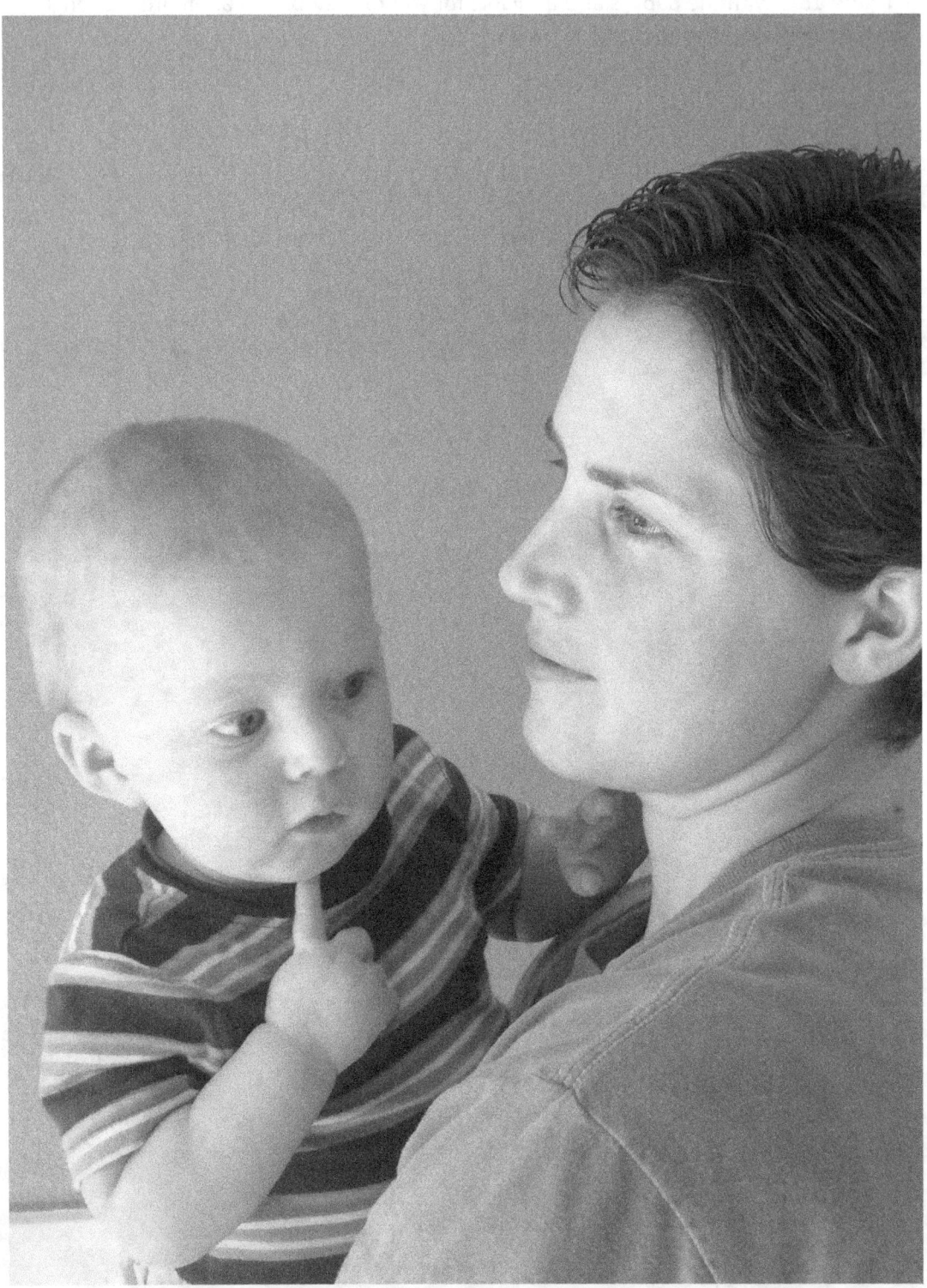

Figure 13-2. Woman in profile view with Baby

Once the picture is chosen, make a grid for it. If it's okay to draw on the picture you can go ahead and do it. If it's not okay to draw on the picture the best thing to use is a piece of clear plastic to place over the picture. Clear slip covers for 8 ½" X 11" sheets of paper work well for this because you can draw a grid on it and slide the picture inside, this way you can use the grid many times.

To make a grid, use a ruler to mark the edges of the plastic or picture using consistent increments. Mark from top to bottom on the left and right sides, and from left to right on the top and bottom edges. To finish the grid, connect the dots from left to right and top to bottom. Depending on the size of the picture you may want to use small increments like ¼ inch or 1 centimeter, if the picture is big you can use a larger increment. Use a pen or fine tip marker to draw the grid, don't use a pencil, the graphite will easily smudge and the grid won't be effective.

If you drew the grid on a piece of plastic you'll need to secure it to the picture using tape. Make sure the grid can't move relative to the picture.

Remember, smaller grid squares will make a more accurate transfer of the image to the paper possible. It requires more initial work but the end result will be better. As your skills improve you can use larger grid squares.

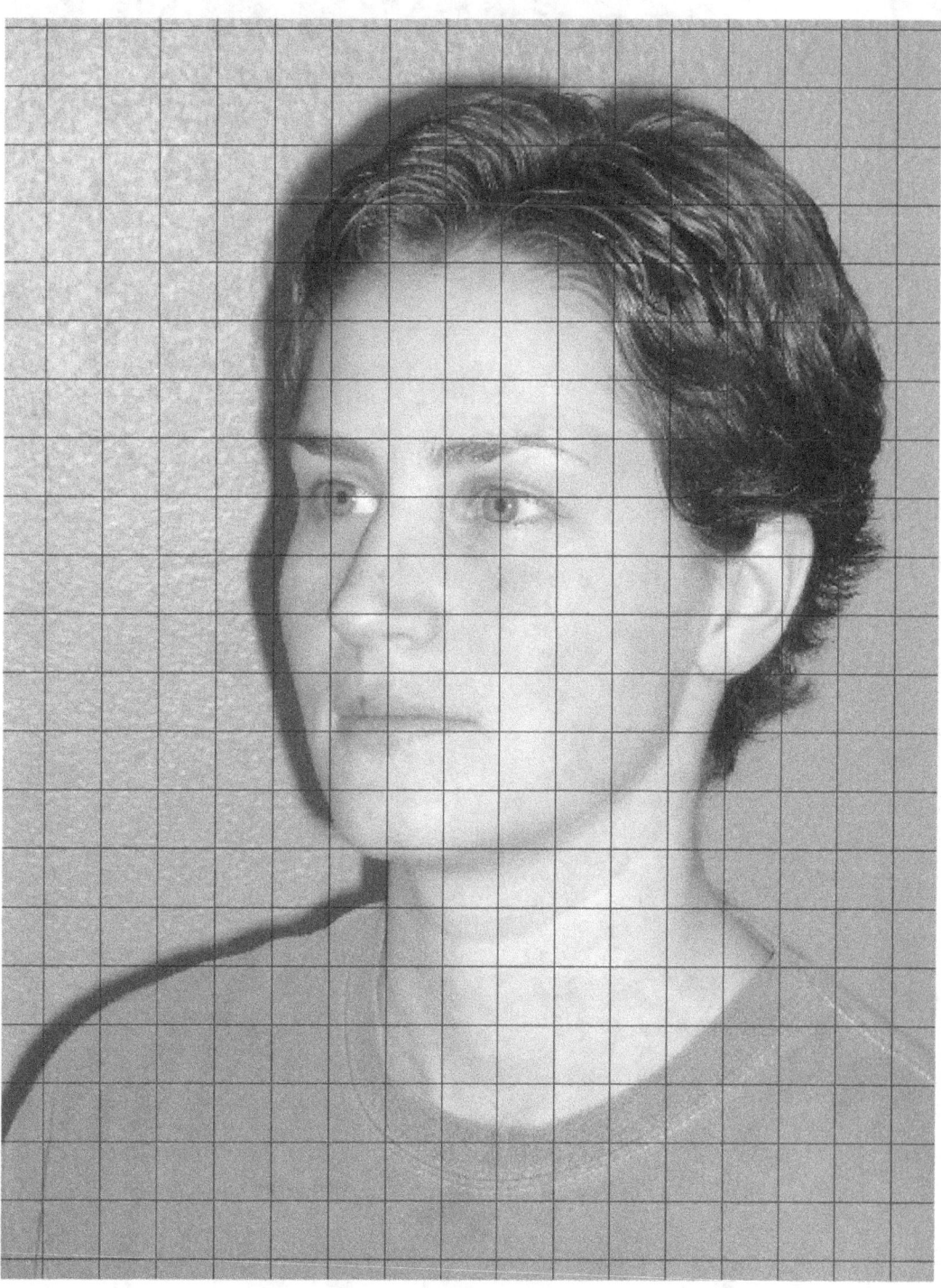

Figure 13-3. Woman in three quarter view, grid with small squares

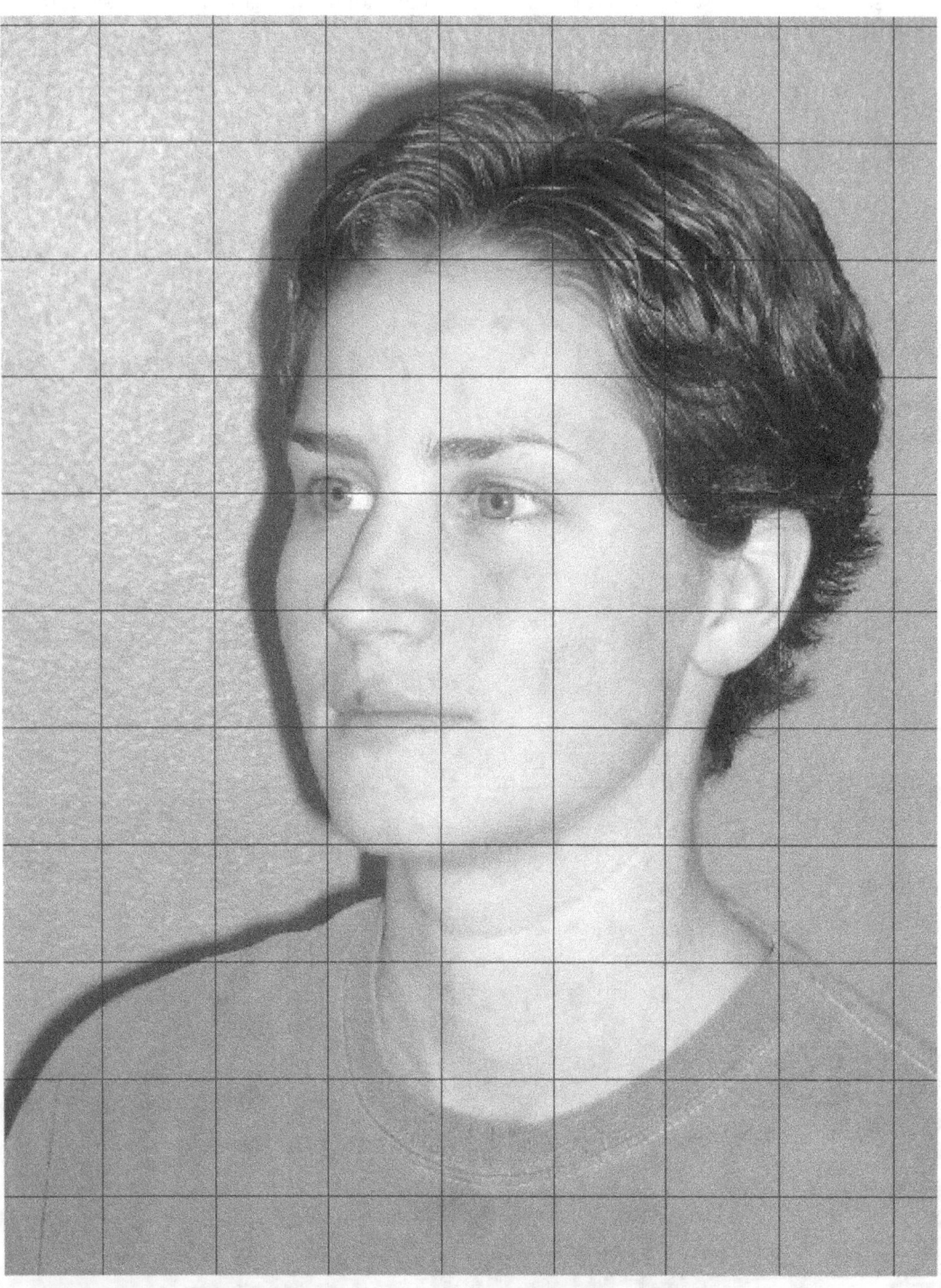

Figure 13-4. Woman in three quarter view, grid with large squares

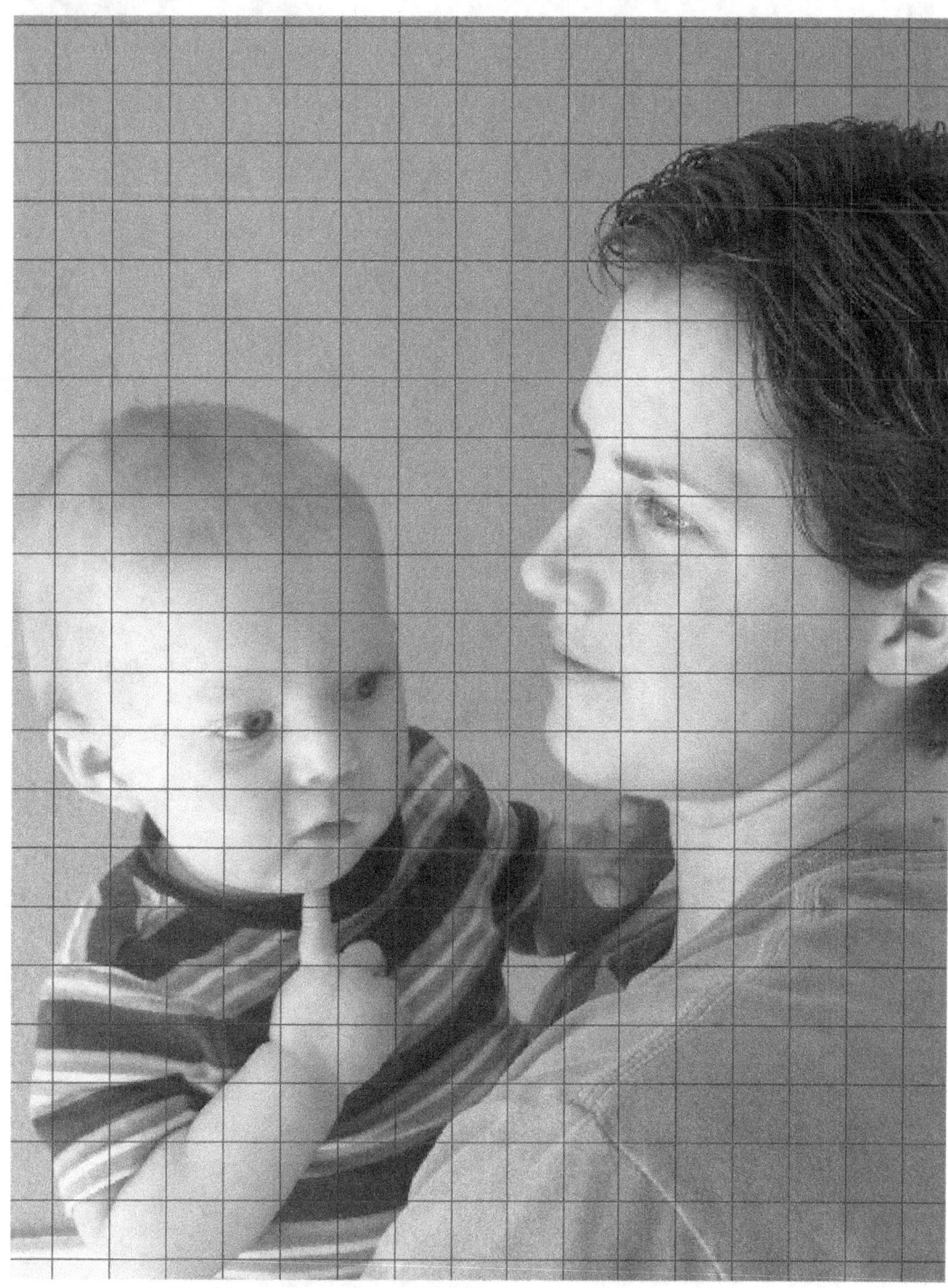

Figure 13-5. Woman with baby, grid with small squares

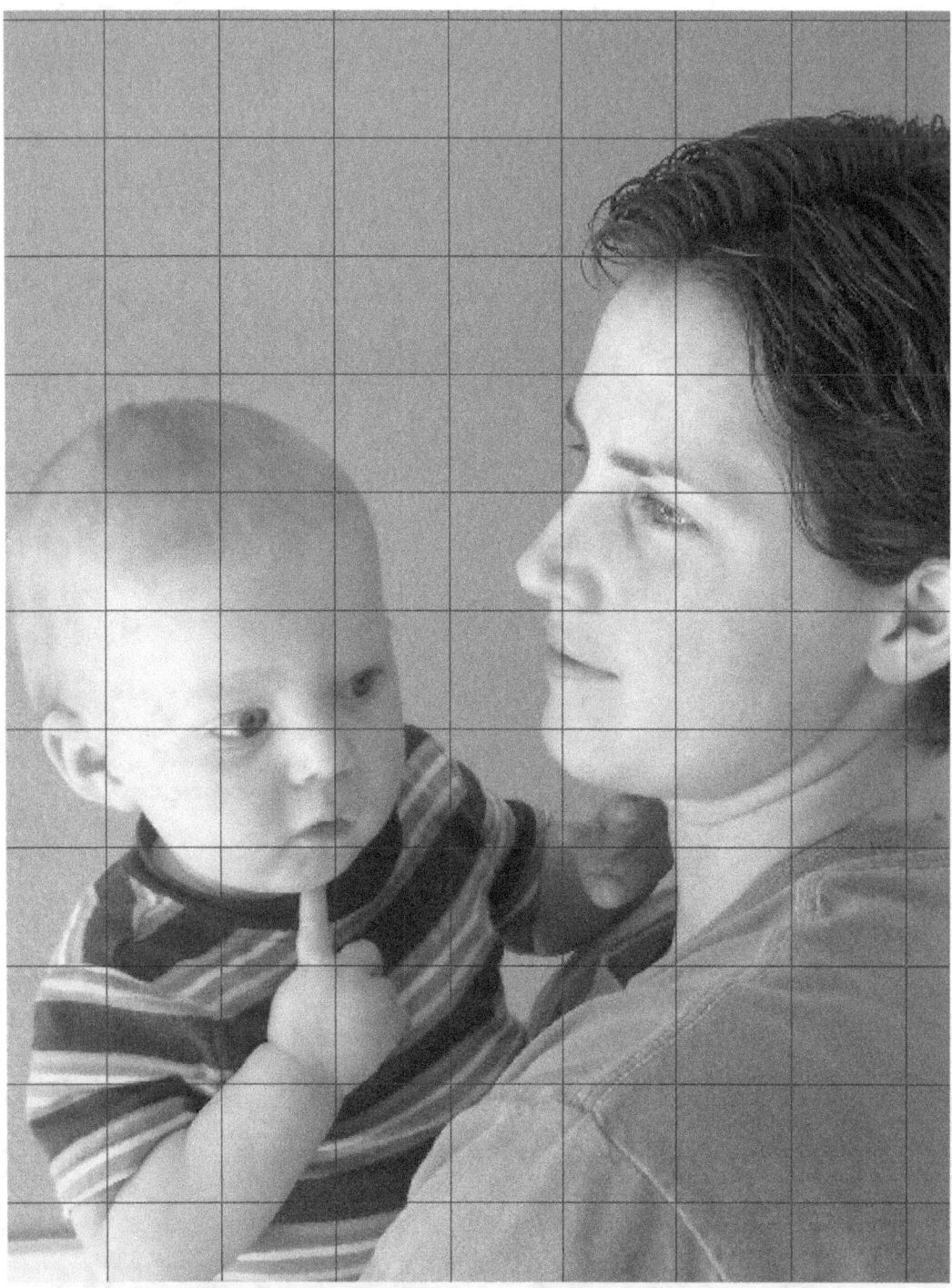

Figure 13-6. Woman with baby, grid with large squares

This time using a pencil, draw a grid on the paper you're going to use for the portrait. Use the same method to mark the paper that you used to mark the picture. Make sure to use very light lines on the paper because you'll need to erase them later.

Note: If your picture is small and you used say ¼ inch grid squares, you can now draw a grid using 1 inch squares on the paper and the portrait will be four times larger than the photograph. You can do the opposite to shrink the portrait too. The increments of the grids aren't important as long as each grid is square. If you want to have a little fun you can change the grid by using uneven increments for example, ¼ inch spacing across the top and bottom and 1 inch spacing up and down the sides. A grid with uneven increments will stretch, skew, or flatten the portrait.

Figure 13-7. Lightly drawn grid with small squares

Step 4.

Transfer the photograph to the paper. Use the grid to help keep the proportions and placement of facial features correct.

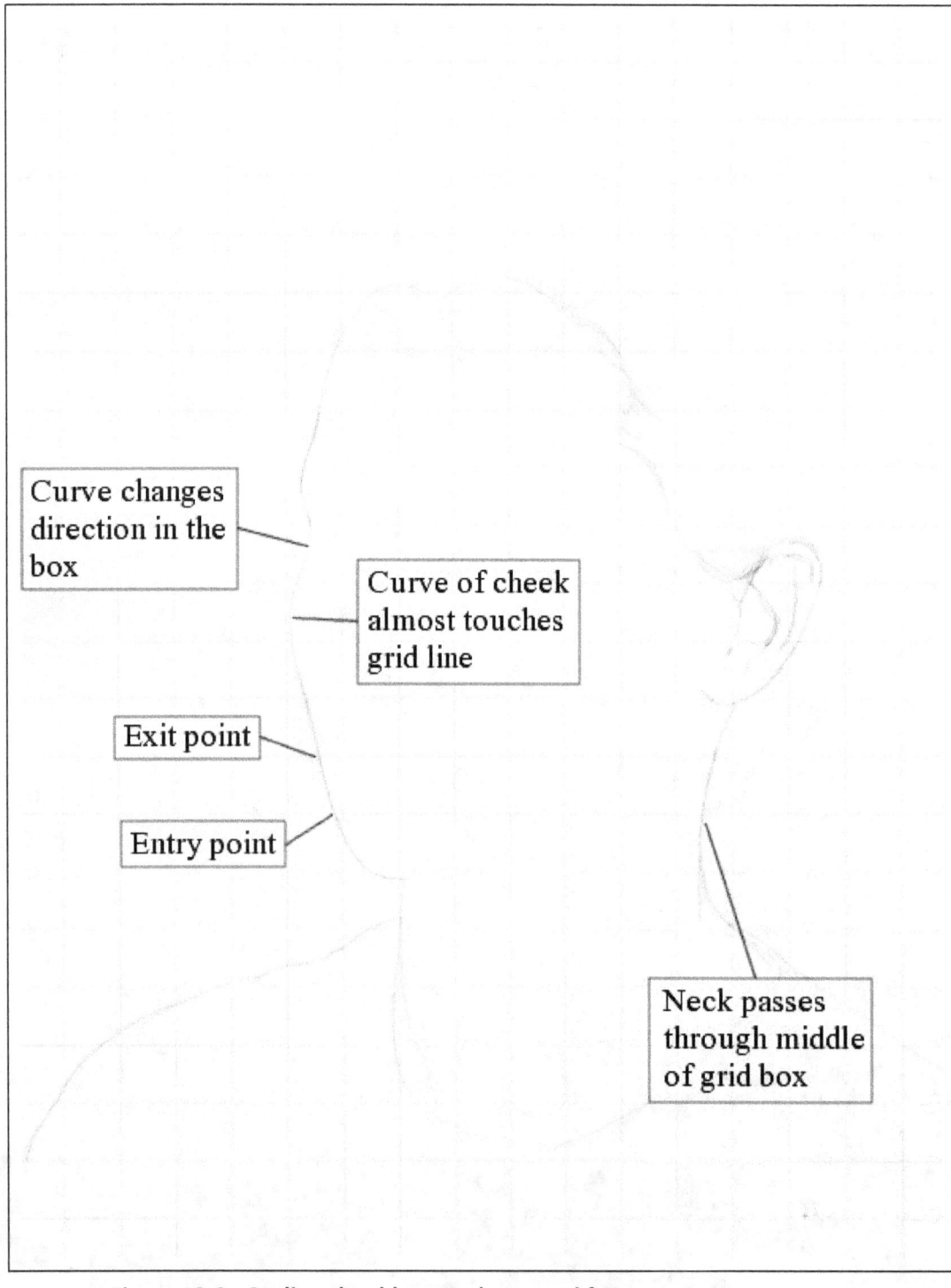

Curve changes direction in the box

Curve of cheek almost touches grid line

Exit point

Entry point

Neck passes through middle of grid box

Figure 13-8. Outline shoulders, neck, ear and face

Find a convenient place to start outlining the head and shoulders. The drawing in this example was started at the base of the shoulder on the left because this point was easy to locate on the photograph and the grid. Starting at the shoulder also gives you time to get the hang of using the grid before you get to the more important facial features.

Facial features will rarely cross the grid at a corner. Your job is to determine where the features cross the lines of each box. Dividing each square of the grid further in your mind will help. Visualize the halfway points and the quarter points of each box as you determine where features are crossing the gridlines. Curves within a square must be estimated as best you can.

Focus on one square at a time.

After you've finished the outline of the head and shoulders, use the grid to outline the major facial features including the eyes, nose, mouth, ears and hair. This is a critical step! Take all the time you need to place each feature correctly, if you don't, the final outcome won't look right no matter how well you do everything else.

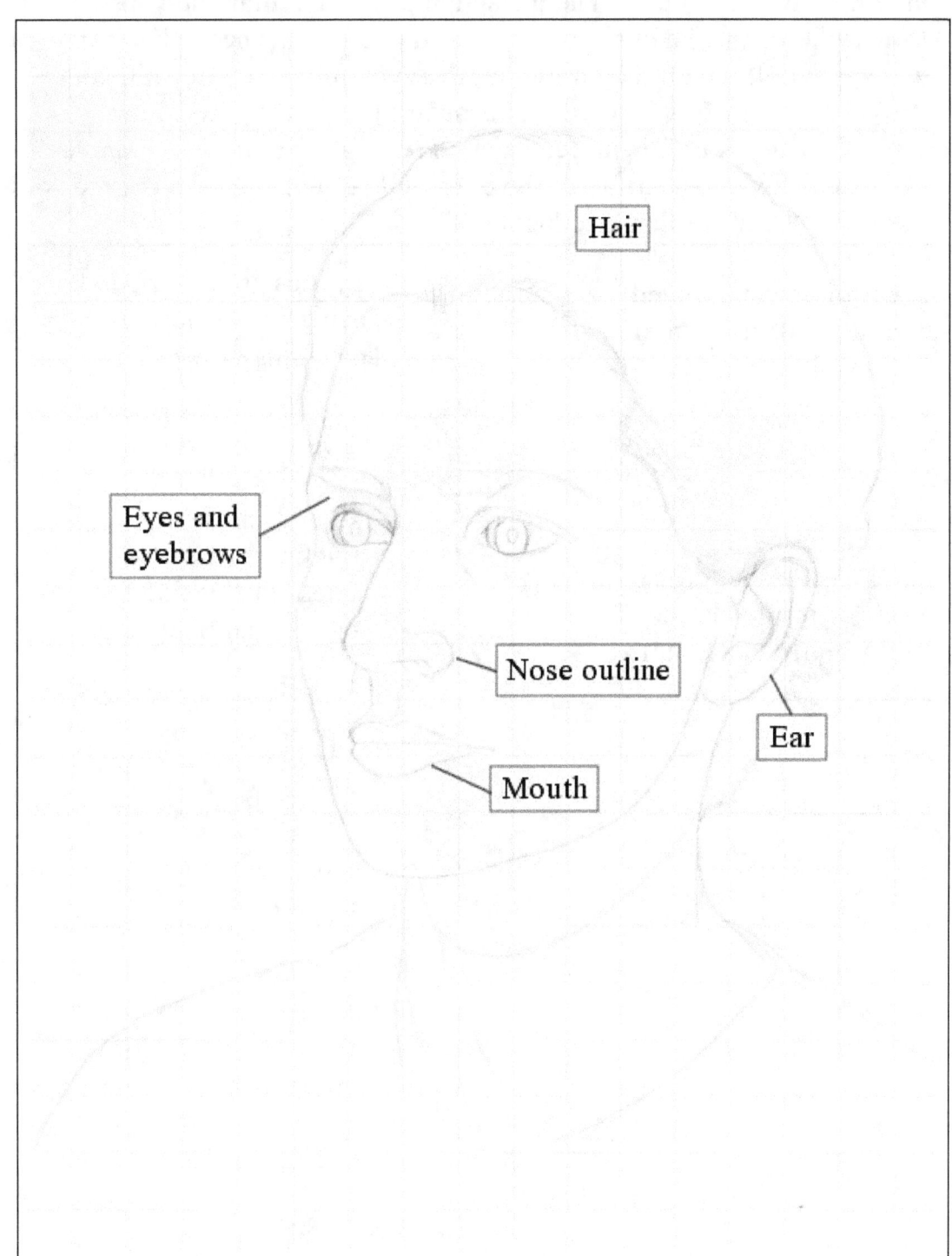

Figure 13-9. Layout of major facial features

Step 6.

When all the facial features are outlined you can erase the grid.

After the grid is gone all that's left to do is add tone. Starting with the eyes, find the highlights; make sure to leave these parts white. Fill in the pupils as dark as you can anywhere there's not a highlight. The color in the iris can be done by adding tone around the edges and blending it in towards the center. The iris is usually a little darker around the edges and lighter towards the pupil. The eyeball is round so the edges will be slightly shaded similar to a sphere. Also, be aware of the eyelid and eyelash reflections, you can't always see them especially if the picture is small, but will want to include them if they're visible.

Eyelids will have highlights that are in line with the highlights of the eyeball. As you add tone to the skin, start at the most shaded areas then use a tissue or tortillon to blend it. Build layers of tone on top of each other, blending each layer until you reach the tone you want.

> Eyes are very expressive and it's important to draw them correctly; take time to study them. The iris and pupil are circular and will follow the rules of a circle when looked at from an angle, that is, they will appear elliptical. The whites of the eye are not really white and will be shaded around the edges because of the curvature of the eyeball. There's usually at least one very bright highlight in the eye because of its moist surface. The eyes will reflect any light source so there may be more than one highlight.

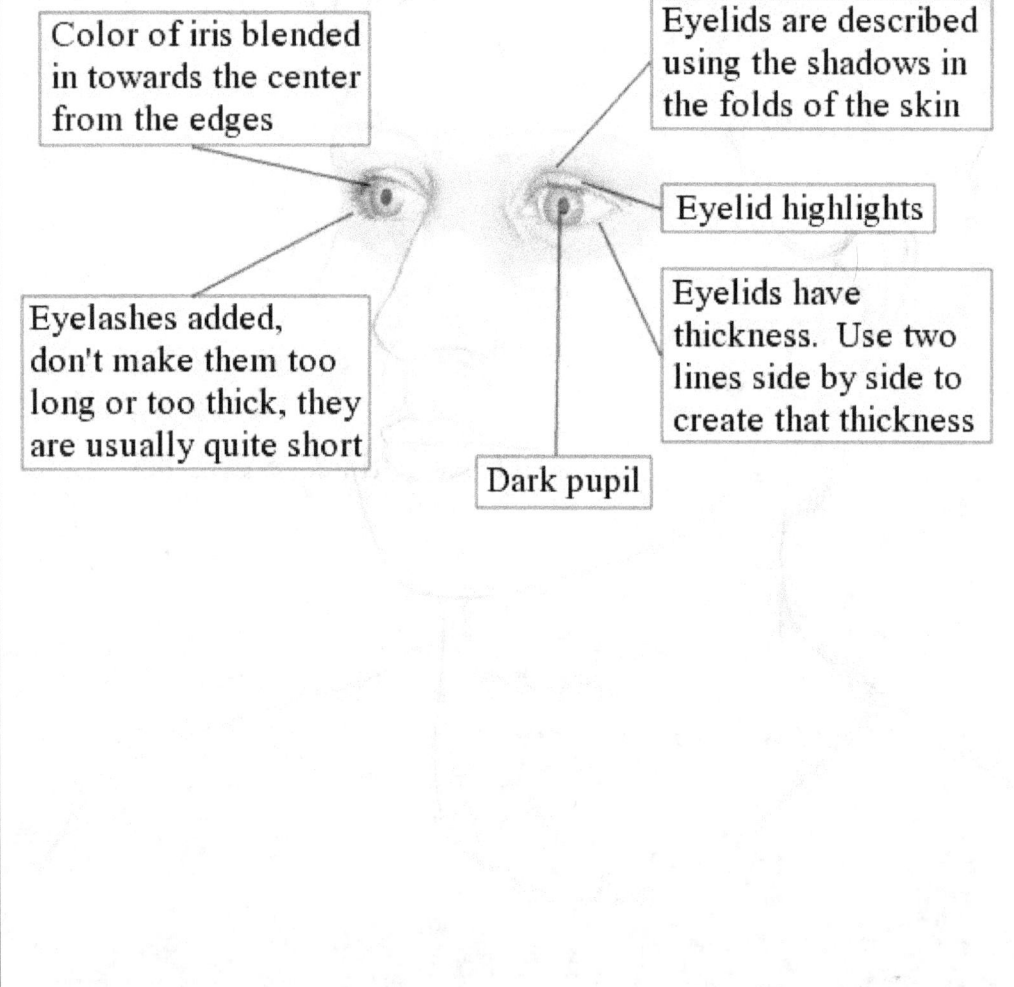

Color of iris blended in towards the center from the edges

Eyelids are described using the shadows in the folds of the skin

Eyelid highlights

Eyelashes added, don't make them too long or too thick, they are usually quite short

Eyelids have thickness. Use two lines side by side to create that thickness

Dark pupil

Figure 13-10. Erase grid, add initial tone to eyes

Use the skin tone around the eyes as a guide for adding tone to the rest of the face.

Carefully observe the picture to determine the areas which have the darkest skin tone and the areas reflecting light. If you need to adjust the tone around the eyes, do that before you move on. After you've adjusted the eyes, add tone to the areas of the face which are the most shaded. Do this very lightly for now and leave any reflective areas white.

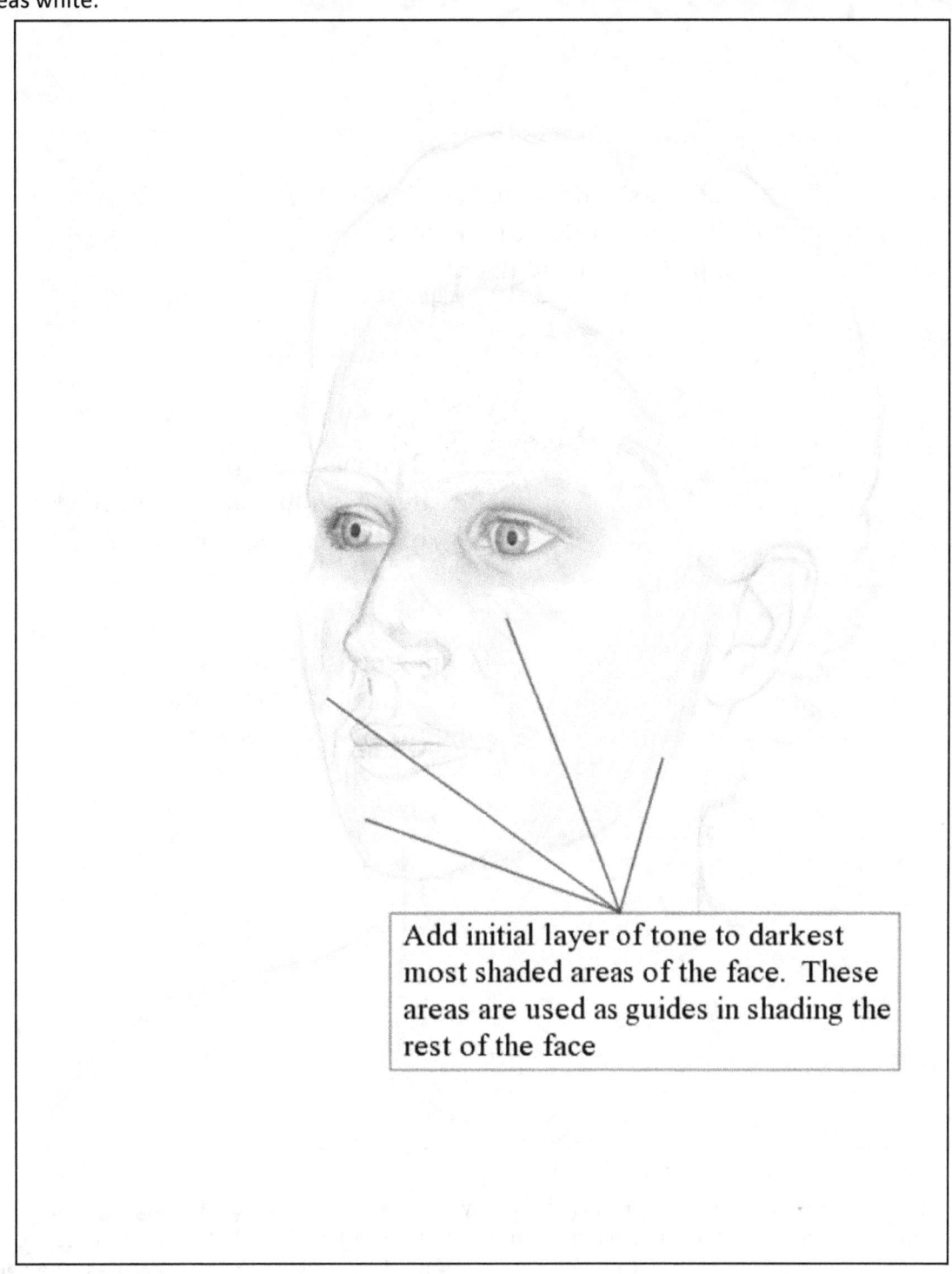

Add initial layer of tone to darkest most shaded areas of the face. These areas are used as guides in shading the rest of the face

Figure 13-11. Initial tone

Step 8.

The nose is one of the more complex features to draw because it protrudes from the face, is an odd shape, can hide other areas of the face and changes appearance when viewed from different angles. The key to drawing the nose is to understand the typical shadows and highlights that describe it. The bridge of the nose down to the tip is usually highlighted on one side. The apex of each ala (the skin around the nostril) and the rim around the nostril are usually highlighted as well. Shading is most common on each side of the bridge near the eye sockets, where the ala meets the cheek, and in and around the nostril opening.

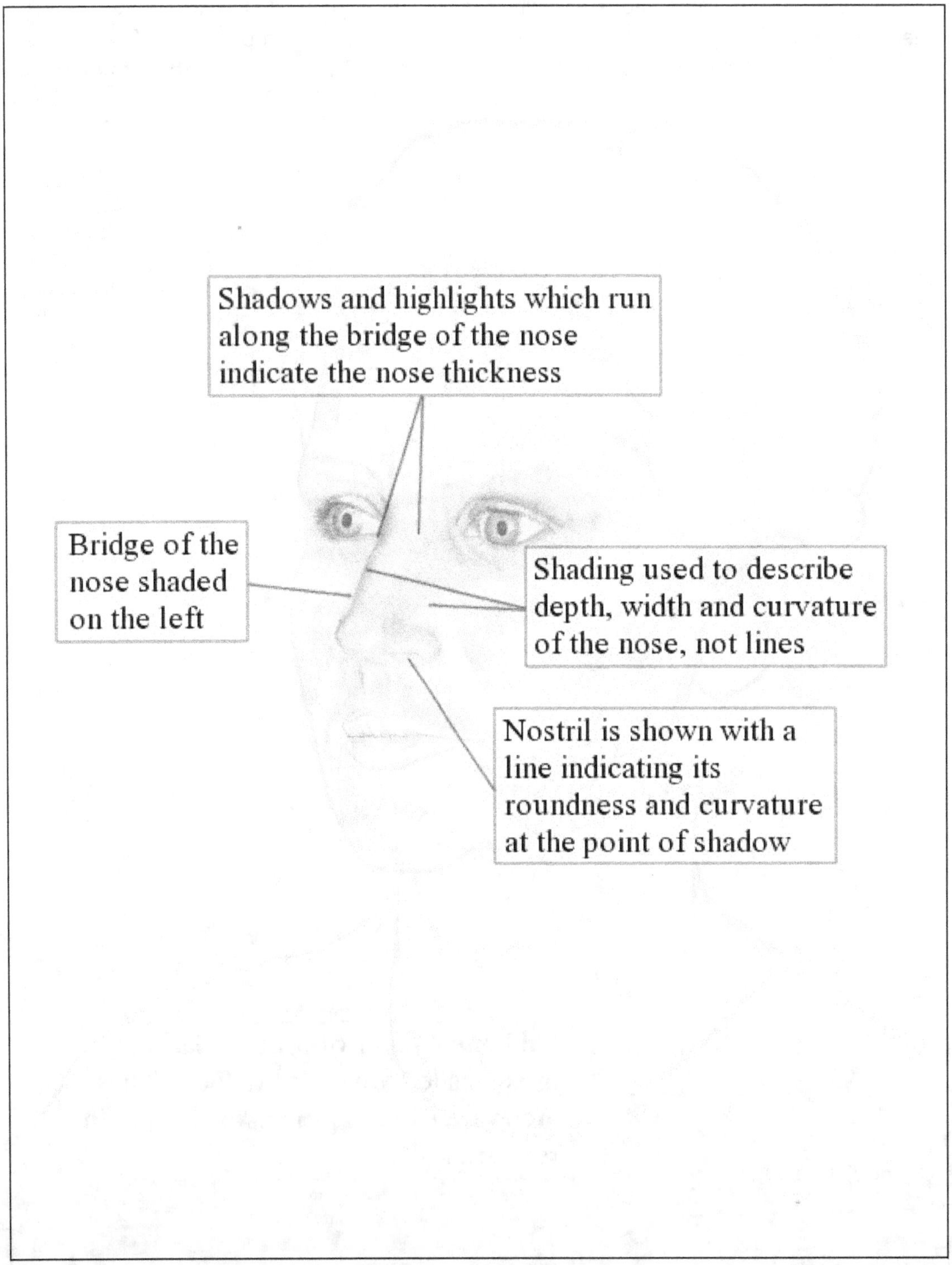

Blend the tone along the bridge of the nose and around the ala where it meets the cheek. Continue to add and blend tone until it matches the depth of tone around the eyes. The right side of the bridge, the tip, and the rim of the ala should remain highlighted as these areas are closest to the light source and viewer.

Shadows and highlights which run along the bridge of the nose indicate the nose thickness

Bridge of the nose shaded on the left

Shading used to describe depth, width and curvature of the nose, not lines

Nostril is shown with a line indicating its roundness and curvature at the point of shadow

Figure 13-12. Blend nose tone

Notice in the example that the bridge of the nose is heavily shaded on the left side and highlighted along the right side. Also, the nostril is not a circle but simply a shaded line. The transition between the eyes, nose and cheeks must be smooth. It shouldn't look as though lines were used to draw any of the features; the variation in tone is what should differentiate them.

When you're satisfied with the tone of the nose add tone to the forehead. The tonal differences of the forehead are very subtle and will be adjusted more carefully later. For now simply add an initial layer of tone similar in depth to the tone around the eyes.

Each forehead is different. Typically the older or more expressive a person is the more details will be in the forehead due to folded skin. Simply drawing lines across the forehead is not correct. Wrinkles must be blended to create smooth transitions into the shaded areas. It doesn't take a large difference in tone to describe a wrinkle, keep them light at first and make them darker later if needed. If there are wrinkles in the forehead, be aware that there will also be highlights along the ridges of the skin folds which must be added to make them look three dimensional.

With the eyes and forehead started the eyebrows can be added too. This can be done a couple different ways. One way is to create a block of tone in the shape of the eyebrow then add various lines and highlights in the general direction of the hairs. The other way is to draw each individual hair. Either way will work; pick the method your most comfortable with.

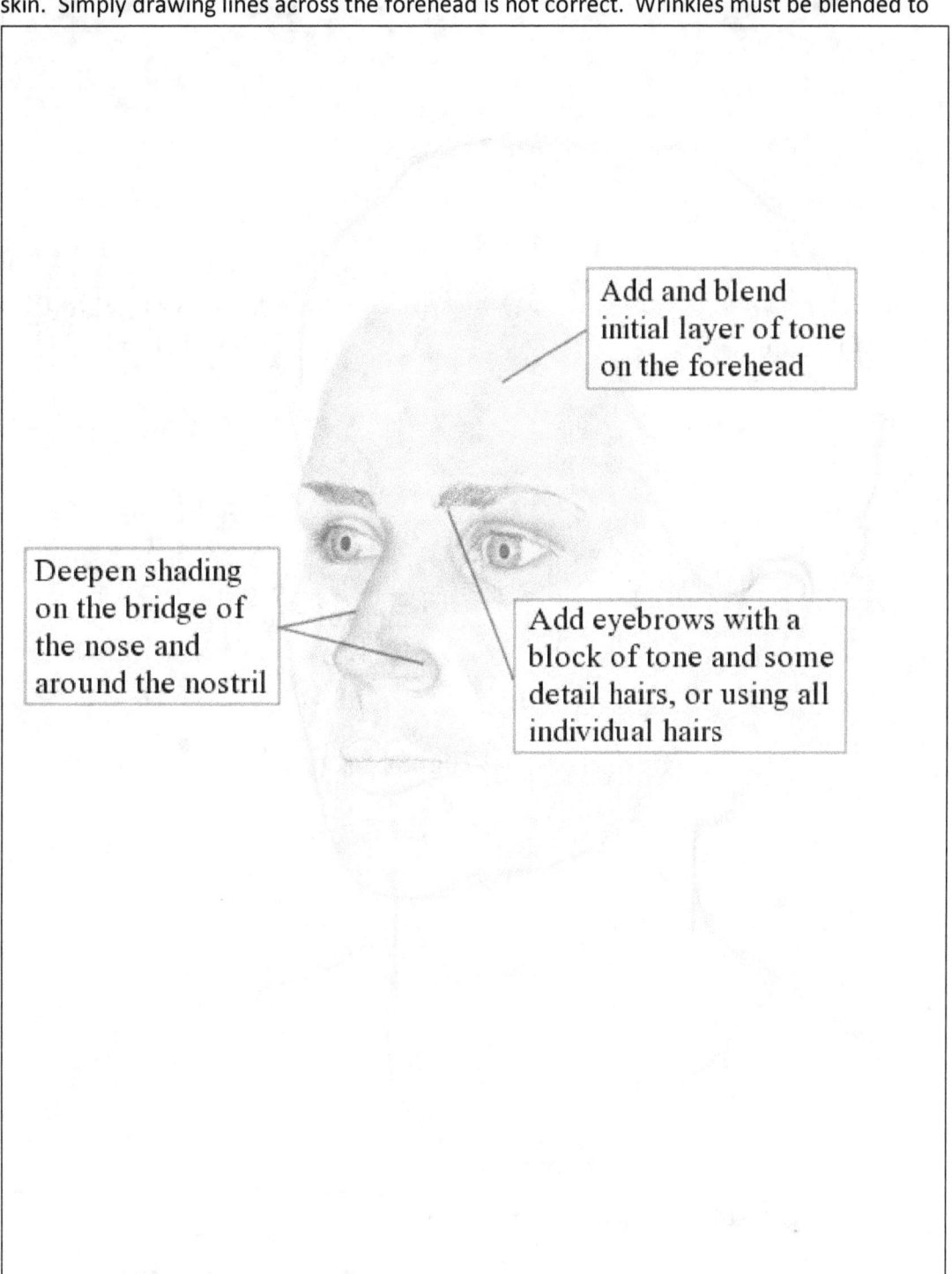

Add and blend initial layer of tone on the forehead

Deepen shading on the bridge of the nose and around the nostril

Add eyebrows with a block of tone and some detail hairs, or using all individual hairs

Figure 13-13. Blend tone for the forehead and initial eyebrow buildup

Step 10.

Finish blending the original layer of tone added in Step 7.

In the example below you'll notice the ridge along the top of the cheek remains highlighted as well as some of the areas where light is reflected around the nose, mouth, and chin. Minor adjustments have also been made to the eyebrows.

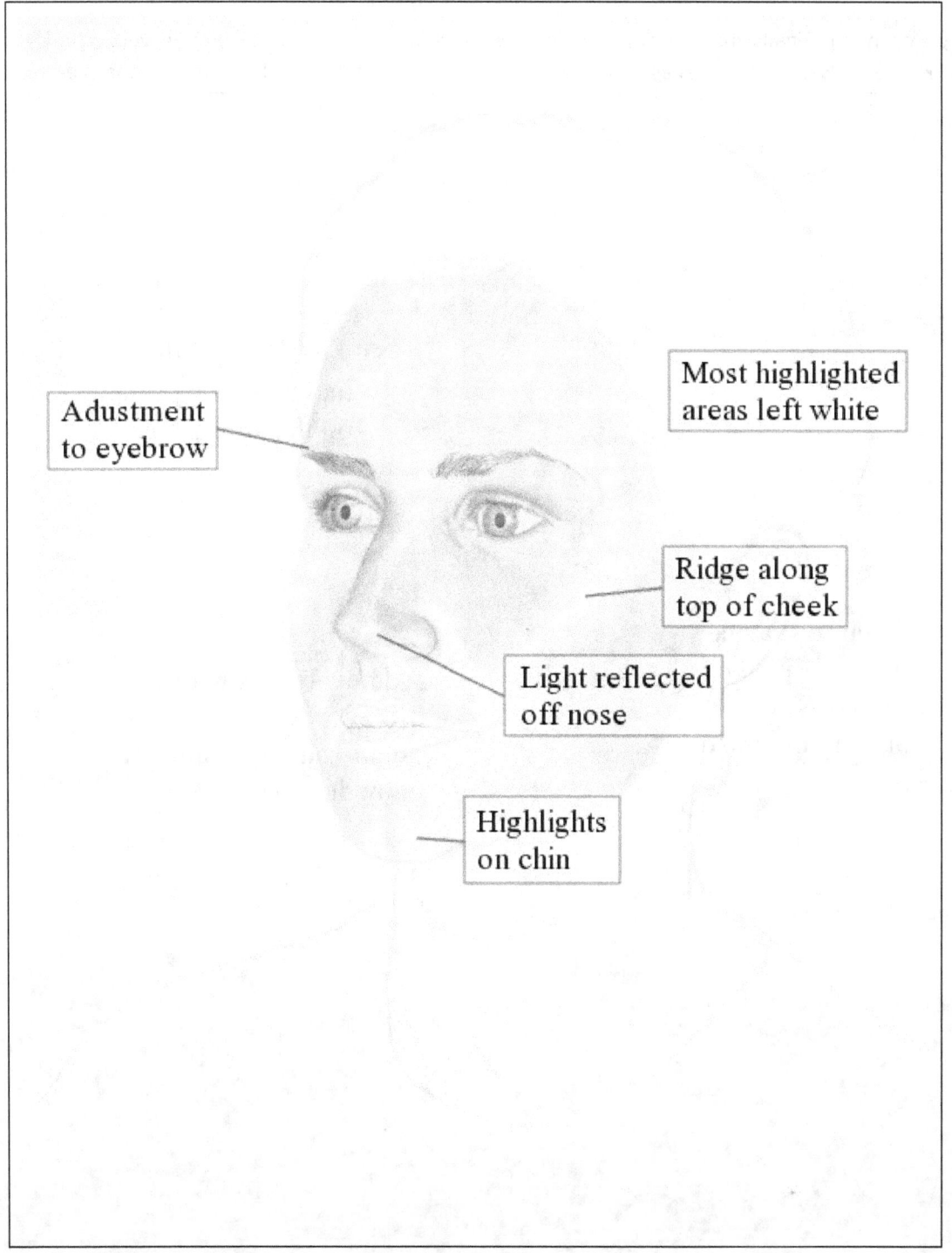

Adustment to eyebrow

Most highlighted areas left white

Ridge along top of cheek

Light reflected off nose

Highlights on chin

Figure 13-14. Blend tone for cheeks and chin

After the initial tone is blended in the face, add tone to the neck and ears. The neck is cylindrical so most of the shading is on the left and right sides as they recede from the highlighted area closest to the light. The neck typically has a few contours which change the shading slightly. Also, similar to the forehead, the neck can have many wrinkles depending on the age of the person and position of the head. Skin folds must be blended into the tone of the neck and highlights added similar to wrinkles in the forehead (see Step 9).

Areas to be aware of include the top of the neck under the jaw and chin, and the bottom of the neck near the shoulders. Shading under the jaw and chin creates the transition between the head and neck. Adequate tone must be added and blended properly otherwise the transition will either be nonexistent or it'll look like a line instead of a transition in tone. It was mentioned above that the neck is cylindrical and that more shading will be on the left and right sides of the highlight. You must also be aware of the possibility of light reflecting off the shoulders onto the neck, this can create a slight lightening effect at the base of the neck near the shoulders.

The ears have many folds and ridges. The shaded areas in the ear are relatively thin so it's important to blend the tone well so it doesn't look like it was drawn with lines. The ear also has many highlights. In this example there are at least five major highlighted areas.

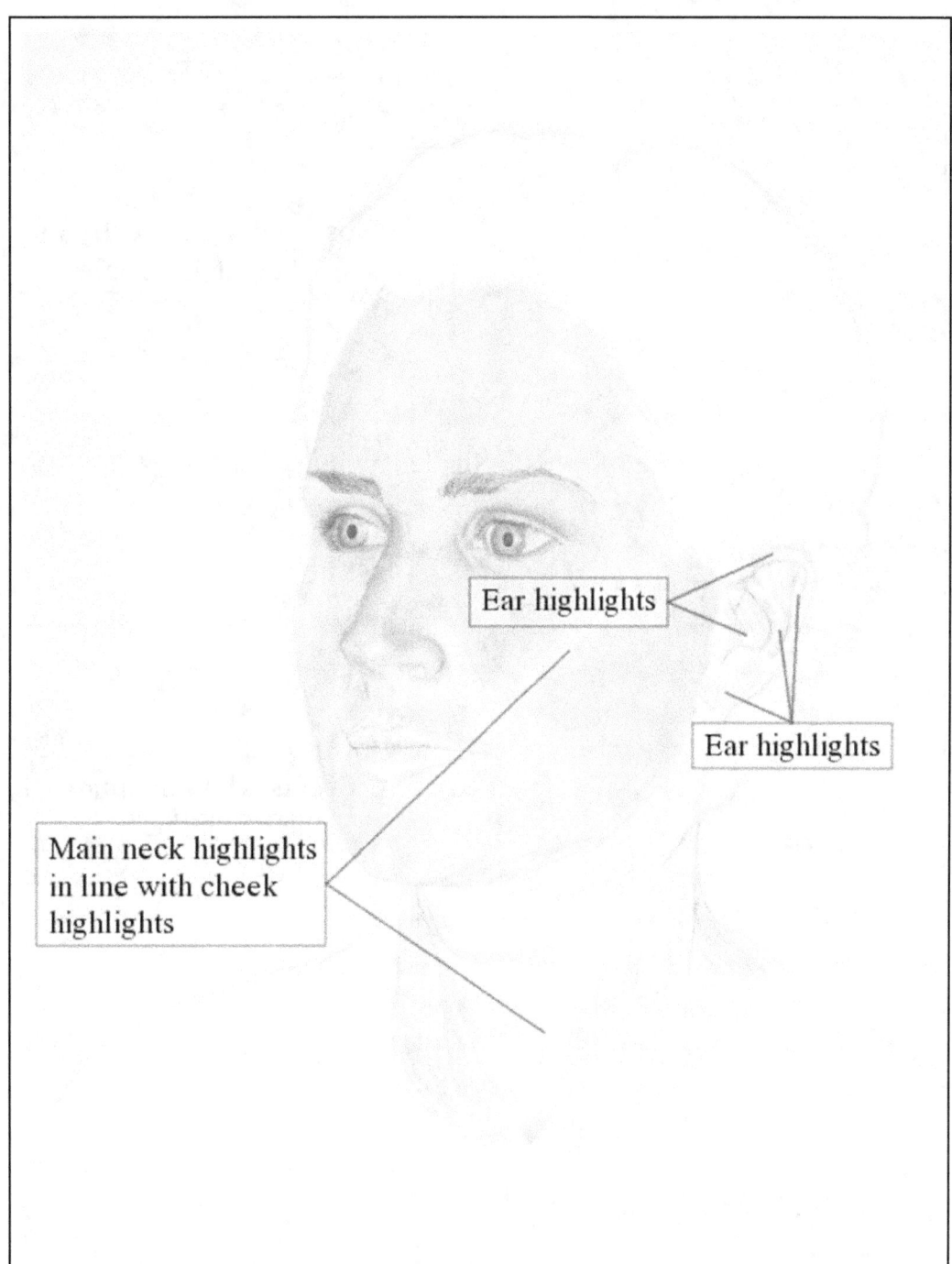

Ear highlights

Ear highlights

Main neck highlights in line with cheek highlights

Figure 13-15. Initial tone for the ear and neck

67

Step 12.

Blend the tone of the ear so it matches the tone of the face. There are many folds in the ear, the highlights and shadows are small and detailed. To blend the tone easily will require a tool with a narrow yet stiff tip, but it must also be soft enough that it won't scratch the paper. Using some tissue, twist one of the corners and fold it over to create a soft stiff surface small enough to control the blending. As you blend make sure to maintain the bright highlights. In a detail like the ear it's easy for the highlights and shadows to get blended together.

When drawing ears, keep in mind they're usually the same length and at a similar angle to the nose. Children's ears seem a bit larger in proportion to their head and the ears of the elderly are typically a little longer than a younger person's.

After completing the ear, add and blend tone along the jaw line to create a smooth transition between the face, ear and top of the neck.

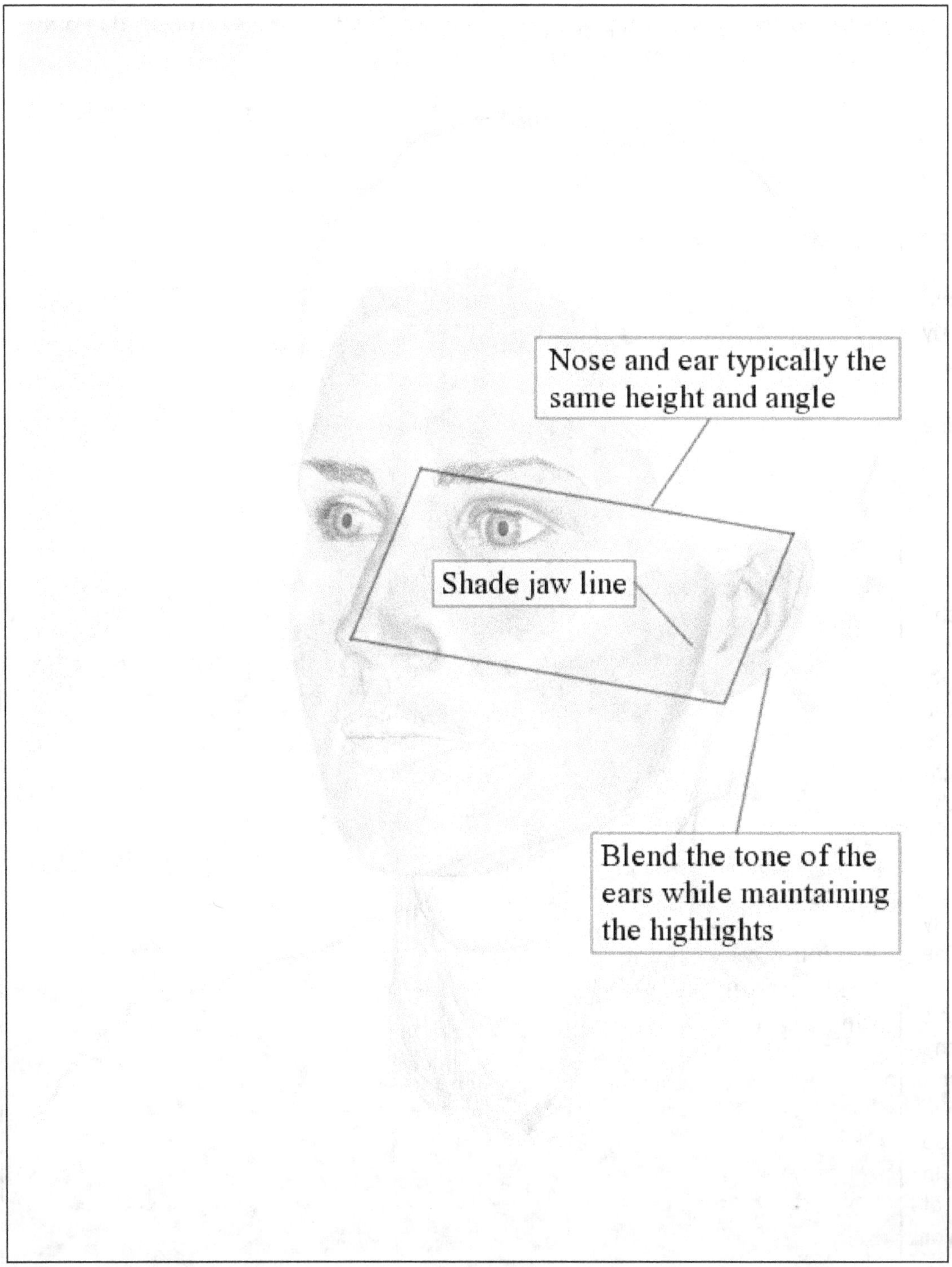

Nose and ear typically the same height and angle

Shade jaw line

Blend the tone of the ears while maintaining the highlights

Figure 13-16. Blend ear tone and jaw line

Move down to the neck and begin blending the tone that was added in Step 11. Most of the highlighted areas will be in line with the highlights of the chin and cheeks.

Pay close attention to the jaw line. Notice there's not an actual line that separates the face from the neck. The skin in that area is what indicates the transition. As the skin goes over the jaw bone toward the neck a slight shadow is created and the tone changes. Develop the jaw line using shading and blend it into the face and neck.

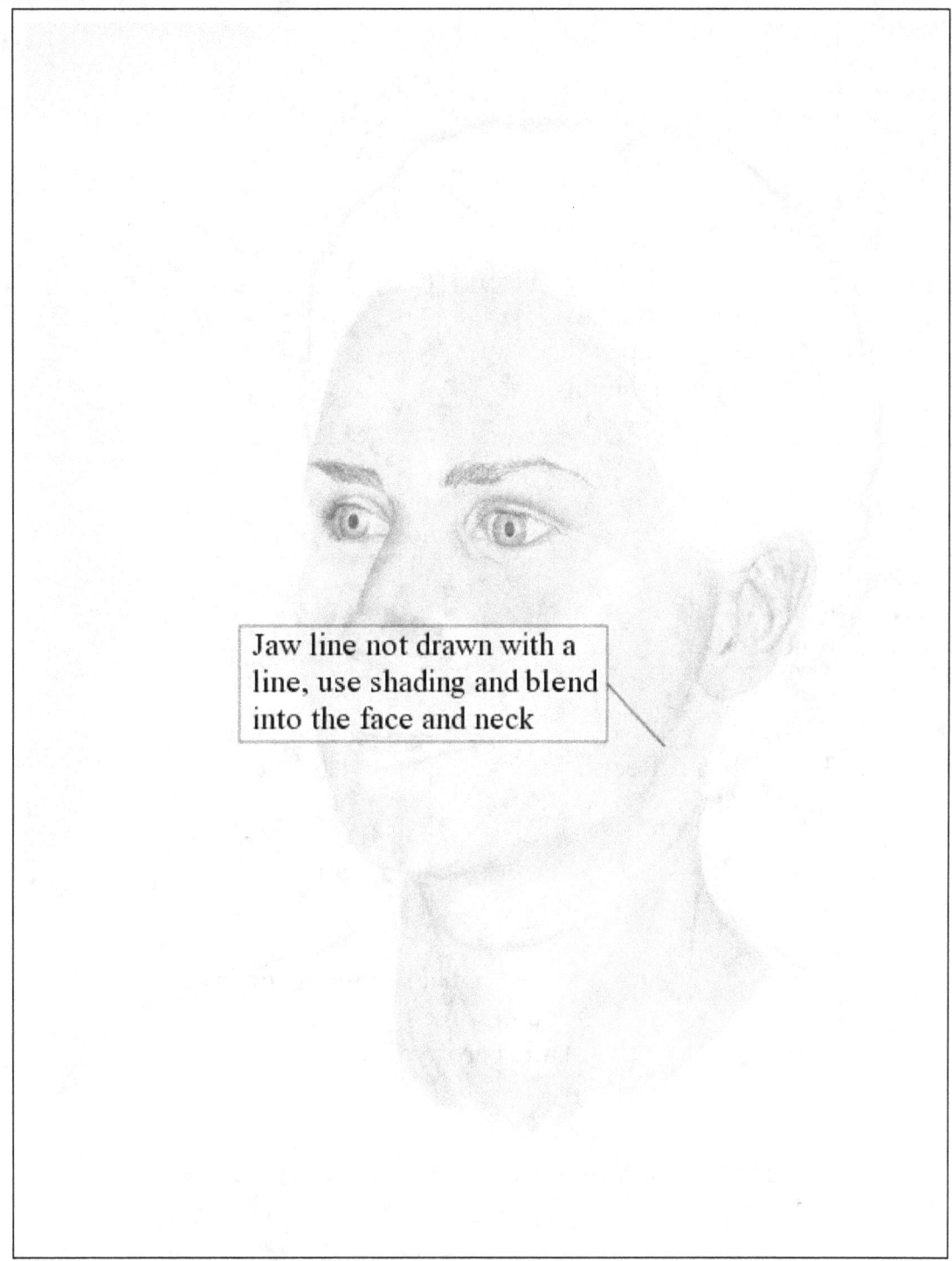

Figure 13-17. Blend neck tone into the jaw line

Step 14.

Aside from the eyes, the lips are the most expressive part of the face, it's important to draw them correctly. Using the grid method you should have a good lip outline already. The next step is to add the tone.

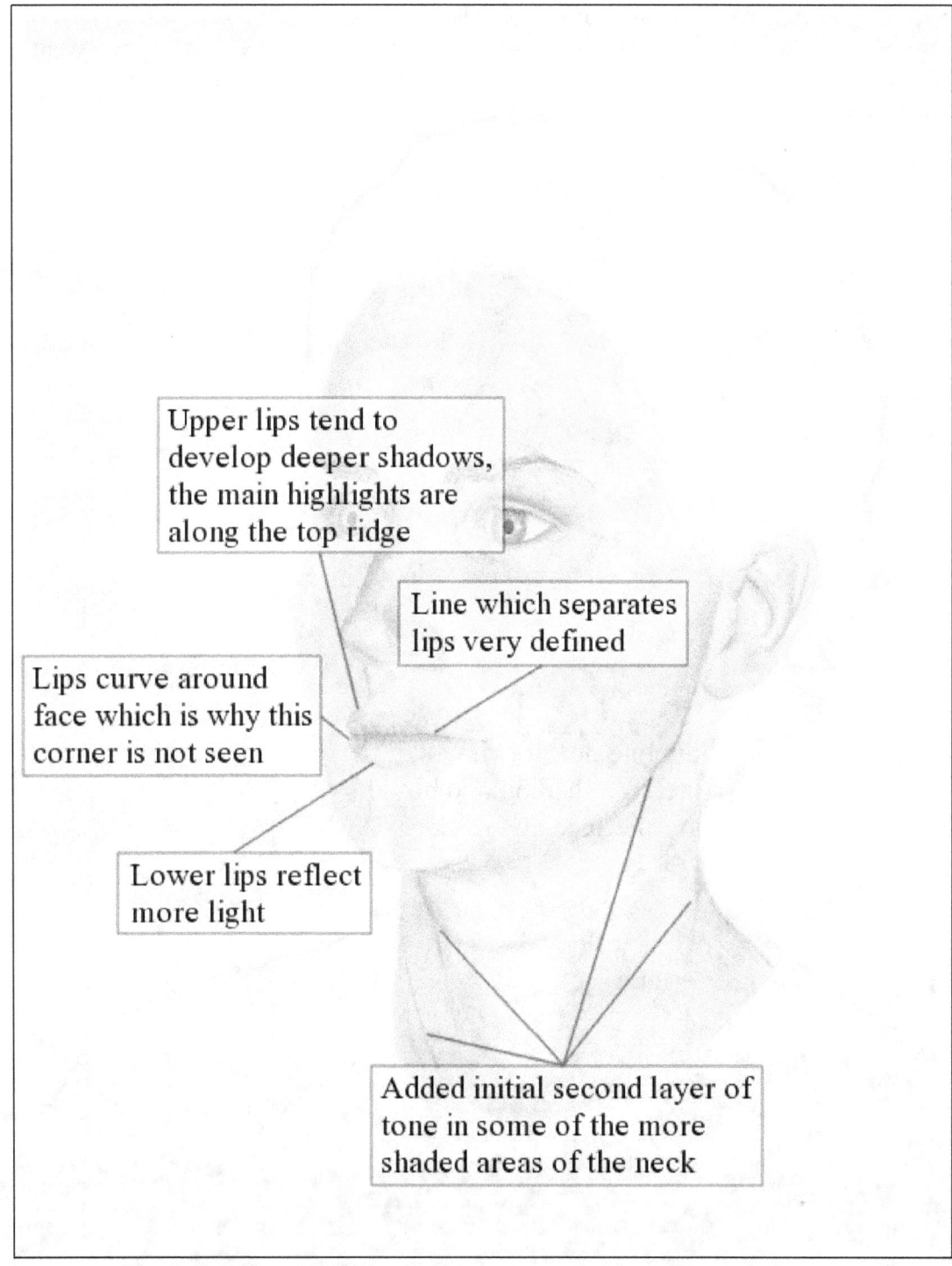

Upper lips tend to develop deeper shadows, the main highlights are along the top ridge

Line which separates lips very defined

Lips curve around face which is why this corner is not seen

Lower lips reflect more light

Added initial second layer of tone in some of the more shaded areas of the neck

Figure 13-18. Blend lip tone, deepen tone around ear, jaw and neck

The line that separates the upper and lower lip is one of the most important lines to get right. If the lips aren't lined up correctly the whole drawing will look awkward. Lips curve around the face so they follow some of the same principles as circles and ellipses. Relaxed lips viewed from below will appear to curve down, when viewed from above they'll appear to curve up. In any view other than full frontal, the lips will be foreshortened which means one side or the other will either start to curve out of sight or be completely out of sight.

The upper lip is typically more shaded than the lower lip so it'll appear darker, especially close to the line which divides the lips. The lower lip is usually more reflective and should have a long highlight along its crest.

All the facial features now have an initial layer of tone, as well as highlights and shading. The next step is to start the hair and clothes.

It's easiest to draw hair in sections as large groups. You wouldn't want to draw each individual hair, it would take too long. Look at the picture to get a general feel for the direction of groups of hairs and outline them as individual objects.

The clothes are not the main focus of this example so very little time was spent adding tone around the shoulders. Any details you add only need to be around the neck line.

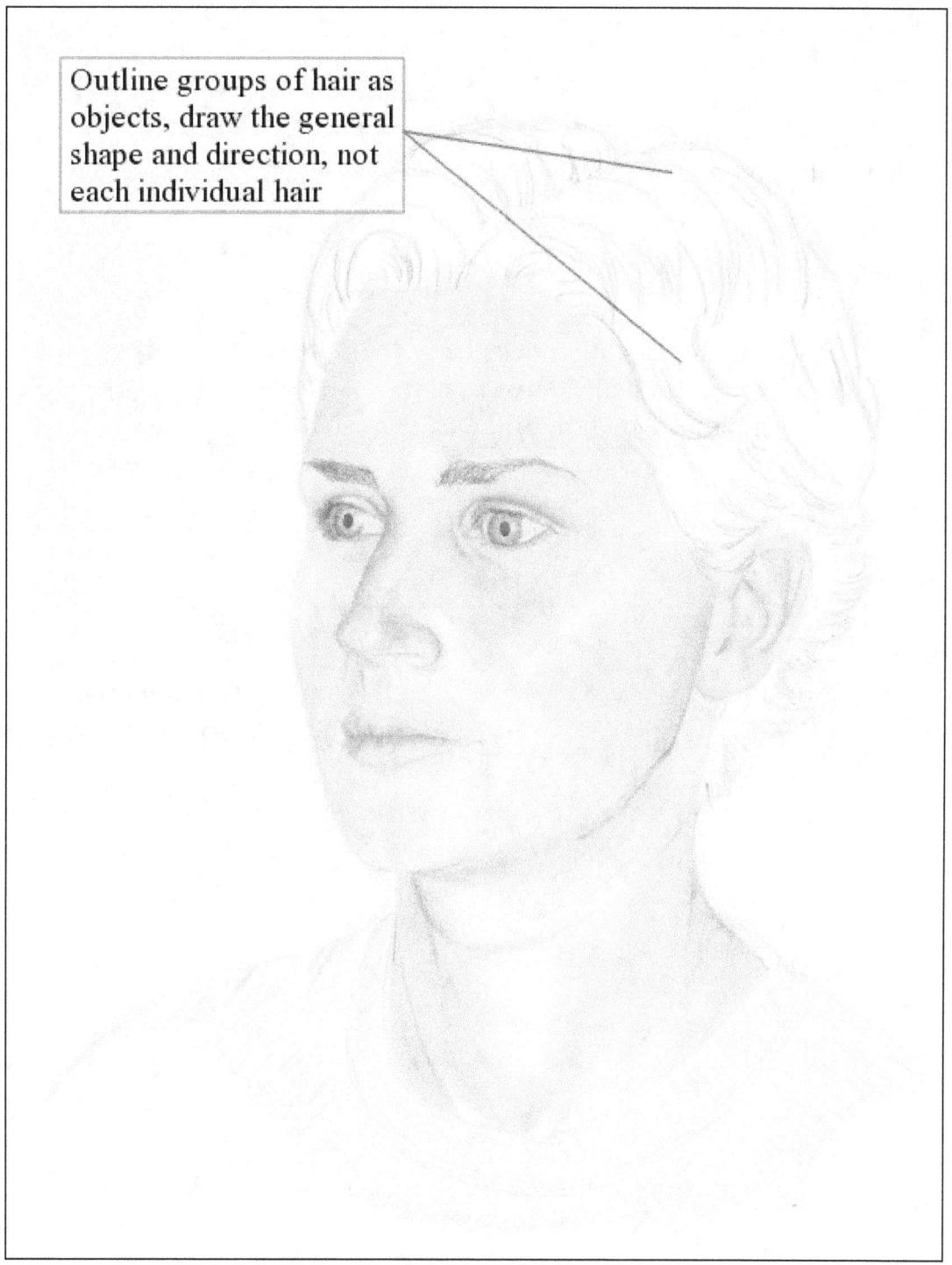

Outline groups of hair as objects, draw the general shape and direction, not each individual hair

Figure 13-19. Initial shirt tone and hair pattern

Step 16.

Blend the tone of the shirt. Add some texture to the collar with hatching and leave some highlights around the rim. Deepen the shadows between the neck and shirt collar.

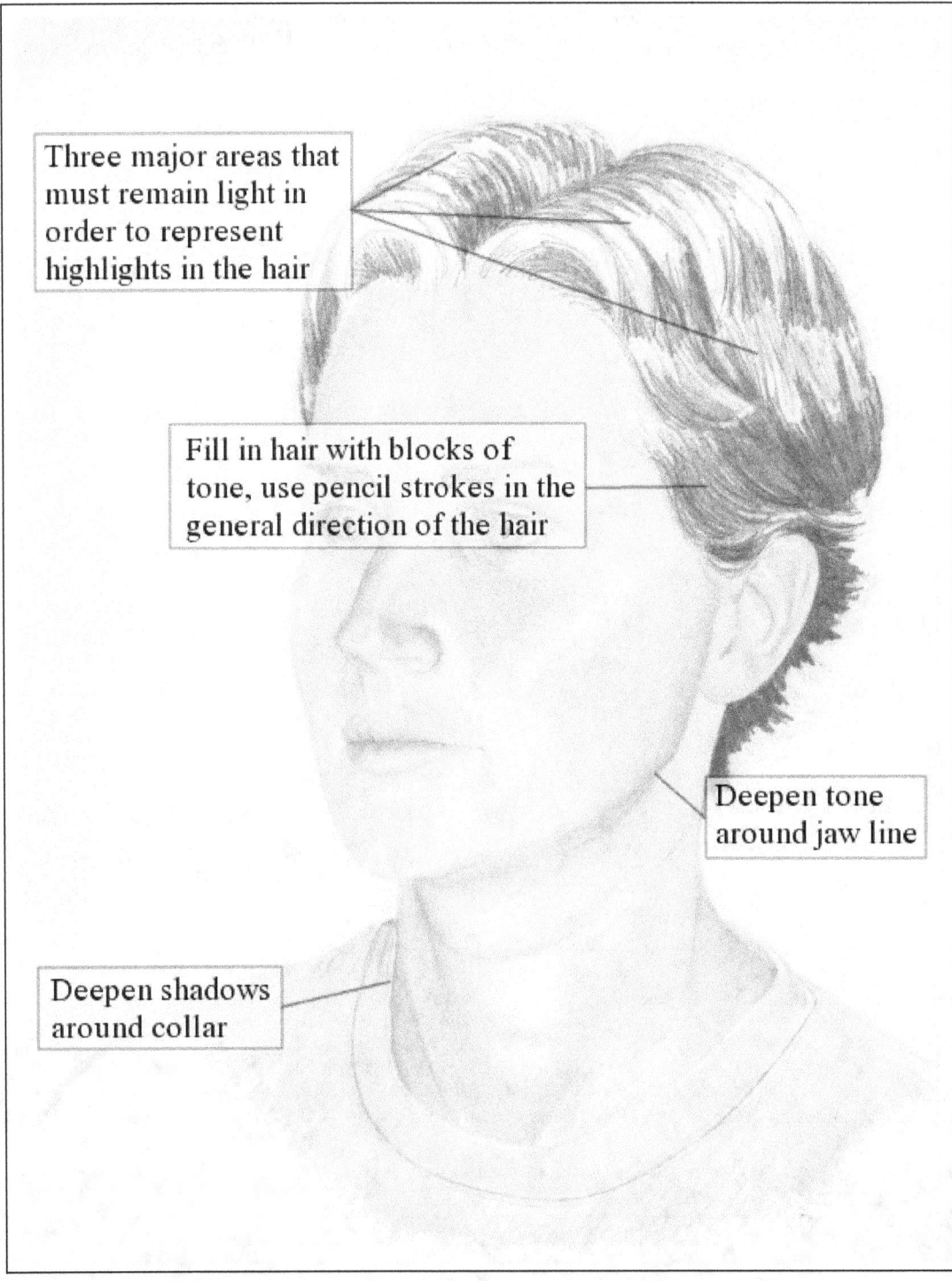

Three major areas that must remain light in order to represent highlights in the hair

Fill in hair with blocks of tone, use pencil strokes in the general direction of the hair

Deepen tone around jaw line

Deepen shadows around collar

Begin filling in the groups of hair you drew in the last step. Again, don't draw individual hairs, instead use blocks of tone drawn in the general direction the hair grows.

Notice in the photograph that hair is very reflective. Highlights generally run in lines along ridges in the head and along the crests of curls. In this example there are three major areas which need to be highlighted, the crest of the hair on the left of the part, the crest of the hair on the right of the part, and along a wave of hair on the side of the head.

Figure 13-20. Blend shirt tone, determine hair highlight locations

When the major areas of tone and highlights have been drawn, finish the hair by adding smaller blocks of tone and individual hairs crossing through the highlights. Use an eraser to create a balance between the highlights and crossing hairs.

Tone has now been applied to every area of the head. From this point on, the task is to adjust the tones shading and highlights to match the photograph better.

Study each area of the face again as you improve the depth and blend of the tone. Make the transitions from shadow to highlight smooth and gradual and match any shadows or tone variations you didn't notice in the initial layout. If the subject's face has many wrinkles this is a good time to explore them in depth and adjust them as needed.

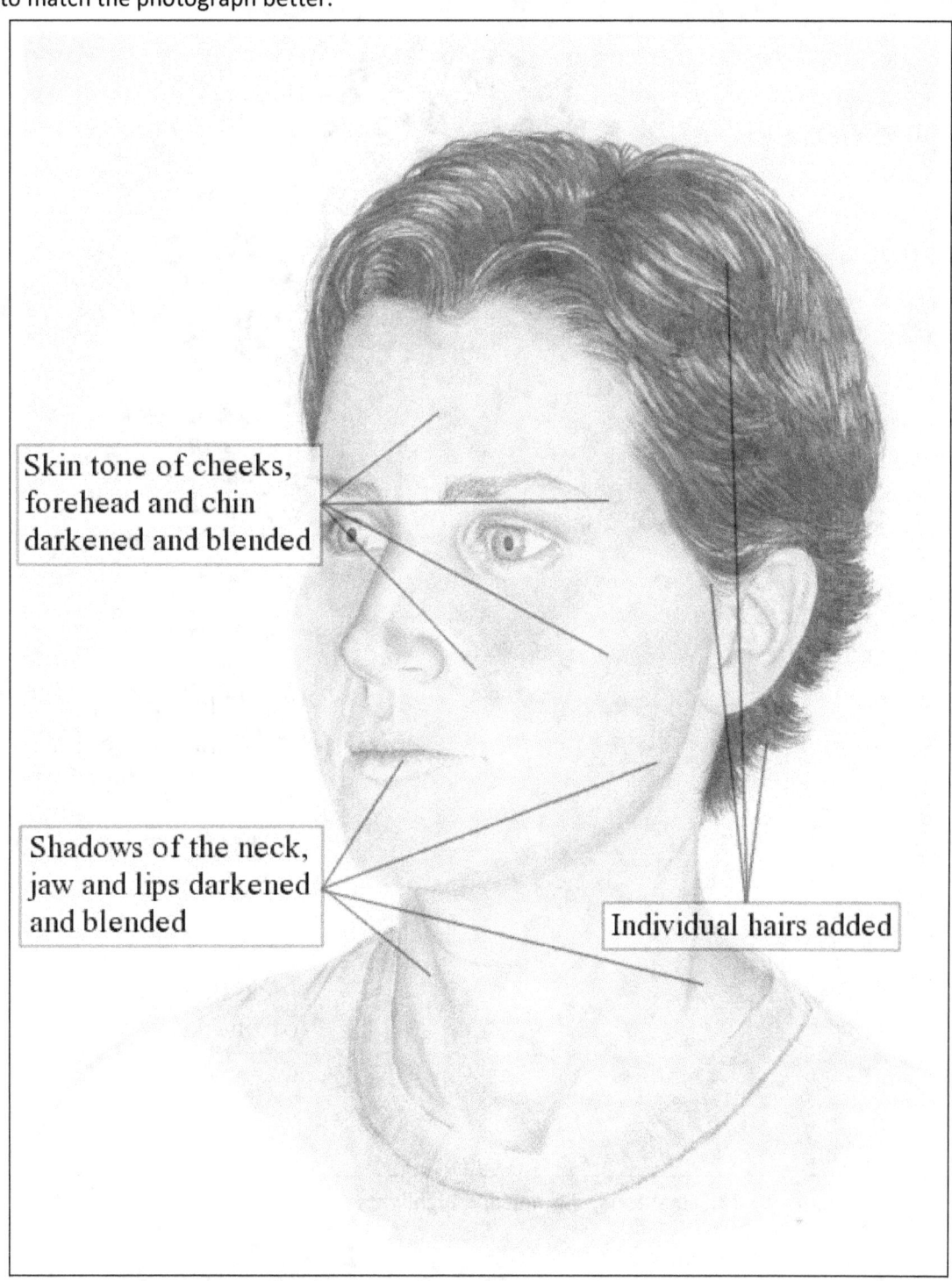

Skin tone of cheeks, forehead and chin darkened and blended

Shadows of the neck, jaw and lips darkened and blended

Individual hairs added

Figure 13-21. Deepen skin tone, detail hair

Step 18.

The final step is to darken the shading and use your eraser to gently bring out the final highlights of the skin. Some of the areas of the face may be too heavily shaded, some might not be shaded enough, enhancing these transitions from light to dark will create a more three dimensional effect.

In this example the lips were shaded and highlighted, the cheek bone was lightened from the nose to the hair line, and the shadows around the eyes were darkened. The shadows on the right side of the neck were lightened and highlights were added. The shading on the jaw was enhanced and blended and finally there was a little bit of touchup work on the hair.

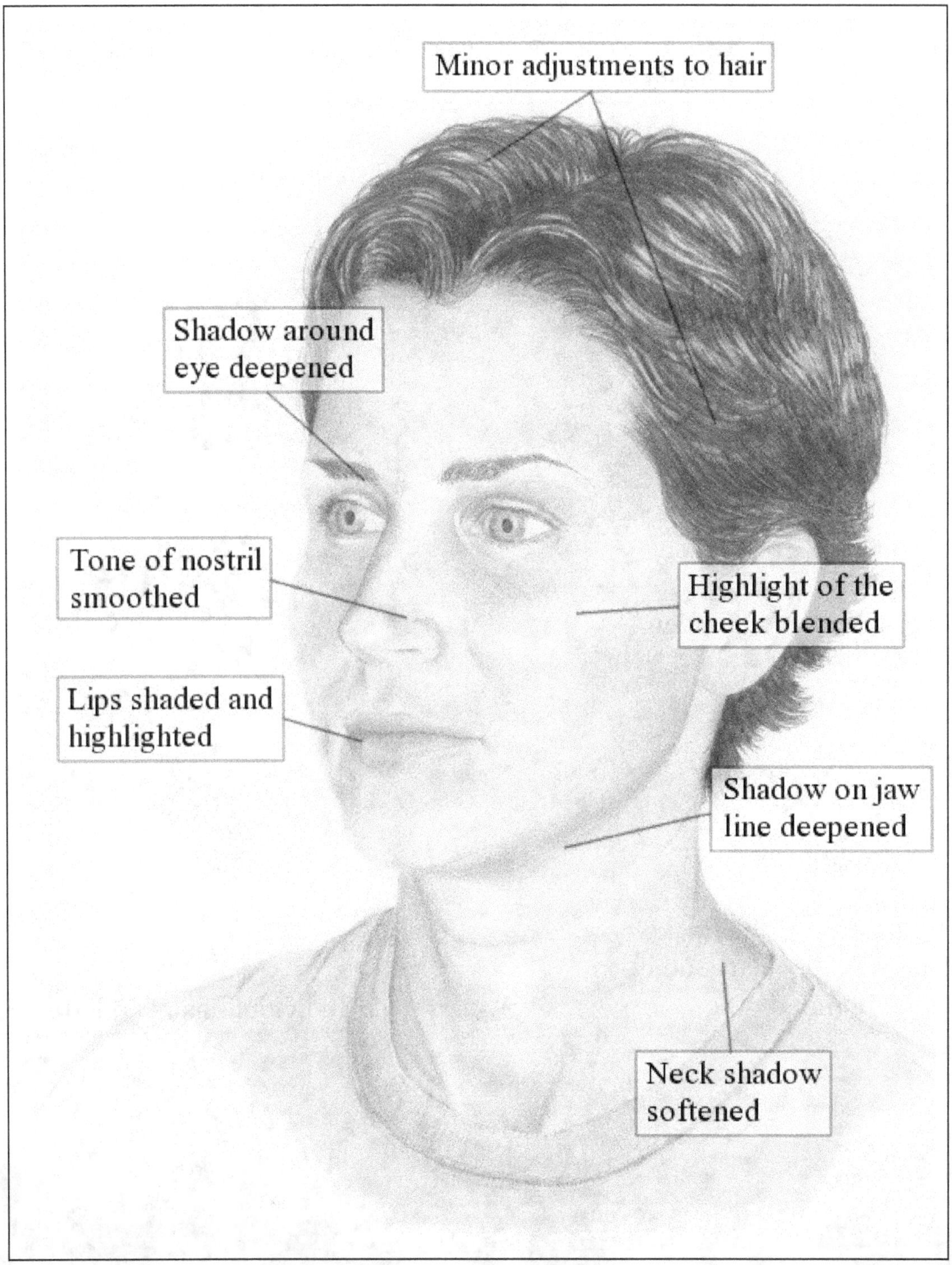

Minor adjustments to hair

Shadow around eye deepened

Tone of nostril smoothed

Lips shaded and highlighted

Highlight of the cheek blended

Shadow on jaw line deepened

Neck shadow softened

Figure 13-22. Final tone, shading and highlights

Results and Comparison

Below is the original photograph along with the final composition done in pencil. As you can see, the grid method helps achieve accurate proportions and position of each facial feature, however, once the facial features have been laid out the accuracy of the final product will come down to how well you observe the photograph and blend the tones of the skin.

Skin is an interesting thing to draw because it has very unique characteristics. Skin is reflective but also slightly transparent; it can be soft and smooth, hard and rough, or loose and wrinkly. No matter what type of skin a person has, blending the different tones is very important. The only way skin will look real is if shades are blended well and highlights are added correctly.

As with anything else the more you practice the better you'll get. Even with the grid method it may require a couple tries to get the results you want.

Don't be discouraged if your first attempt at using the gird method, or at drawing a person in general, doesn't turn out well. As you use this method and learn the details of a person's individual features you'll be able to use that knowledge to draw a more accurate representation the second or third time if you choose to do so. The more you practice the better you'll get at producing an accurate portrait on the first attempt.

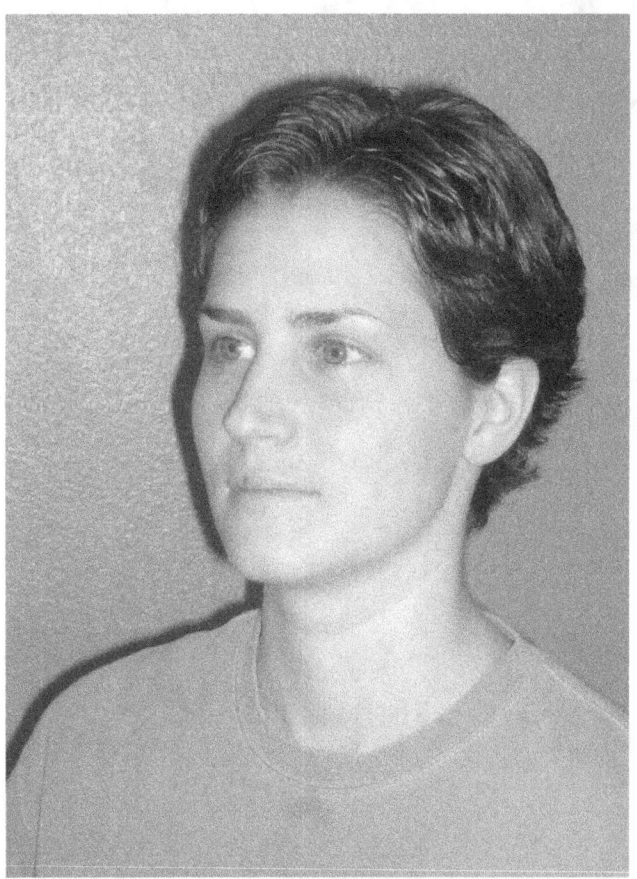 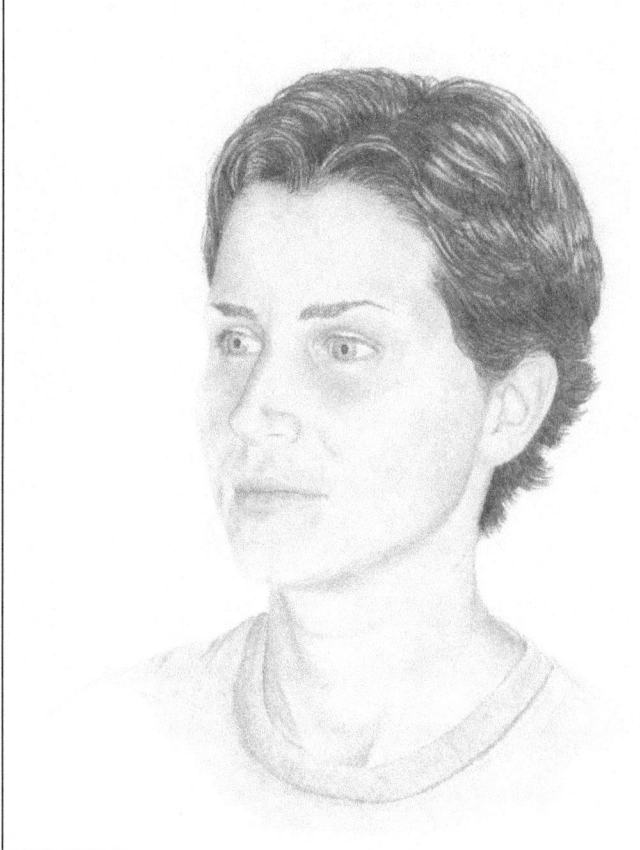

Figure 13-23. Photograph vs. final drawing

Conclusion

You've now finished Volume 13 in which you've learned the necessary skills to accurately transfer a portrait onto paper. With persistence and practice your skills at drawing people will continue to improve. Hopefully you'll be able to share this skill with people you care about. You'll find it to be an enjoyable and rewarding experience. If you feel you still need more guidance on the subject of drawing people, refer to Volume 9; in it you'll find more information that may help you. There are also numerous other books on the subject of drawing people, you're encouraged to seek those out as well. There's always something more to learn about the human face as each one is different, so if you want to be good at drawing it, continue to learn as much as you can and draw it as often as possible.

www.ingramcontent.com/pod-product-compliance
Lightning Source LLC
Chambersburg PA
CBHW081556170526
45166CB00009B/2720